Lucia E. Parent

Beagles

Everything About Purchase, Care, Nutrition, Handling, and Behavior

Filled with Full-color Photographs

Illustrations by Michele Earle-Bridges

BARRON'S

2 CONTENTS

Considerations Before You Buy 5

Is a Beagle Right for You? 5
Space Considerations 6
The Dog Trade 7
Selecting a Breeder 7
Selecting a Puppy 10
Taking the Puppy Home 11
HOW-TO: Basic Training 14

Basic Rules of Beagle Care 17

Getting the Puppy Settled 17
A Private Spot 17
The Doghouse 18
The Run 19
Boarding Kennels 19
Traveling with Your Beagle 22
The Security Room 22
Toys—Good and Bad 22
Beagles and Children 23
HOW-TO: Choosing Equipment 26

Grooming 29

Care of the Teeth 29
Foot Care 29
Care of the Nails 30
The Ears 31
Fleas 34
Lice 35
Ticks 35
HOW-TO: Coat Care 38

The Proper Diet 41

Meat 41
Carbohydrates 42
Fats and Oils 43
Vitamins and Minerals 43
Commercial Dog Food 43
Feeding Puppies 45
Feeding Growing Dogs 47
Feeding the Grown Dog 47
Feeding Pregnant Dams 47

Raising Beagles 49

Estrus, and What to Do About It 49
The Stud 50
Mating 50
Pregnancy 50
Preparations 51
Birth 53
The Checkup 55
Cesarean Operations 56
Nursing 56
Caring for the Puppies 57
Leave-taking 59

If Your Beagle Gets Sick 61

Disorders of the Coat and Skin 61
Disorders of the Digestive System 62
Worms 63
Kennel Cough 65
Serious Diseases 66
First Aid 69
Pulse and Heartbeat 71
Euthanasia 71

Simple Obedience Training   73

Basic Obedience for Pets   73

Understanding Beagles   81

History   82

Beagles for Work in
the Field   83

Beagle Shows   86

Information   90

Index   94

CONSIDERATIONS BEFORE YOU BUY

There are many good reasons to acquire a beagle. Just be sure this popular hound will be right for you.

Is a Beagle Right for You?

A beagle is not an easy pet to keep. It requires a lot from you. You have to remain devoted for 12 to 15 years or more and provide constant good, and therefore expensive, care.

If other people will be involved, you have to be sure that they are emotionally and reasonably prepared to take on a beagle and understand what will be required of them. The person who will bear the primary responsibility for the chores of maintaining the dog should get first consideration.

If the decision to buy a puppy isn't properly made, the dog is going to be the biggest loser. Generally what happens is that the poor puppy is sent from one family that is not prepared to care for it to another equally unprepared. It winds up neurotic and unmanageable.

The beagle is not only gentle and lovable, but also very responsive, naturally curious, alert, and intelligent. It has an even temperament.

One Beagle or Two?

Another point to consider may surprise you: perhaps you ought to get *two* beagles! Remember, beagles are pack dogs. If you think that your work or other duties may keep you from spending enough time with your dog, two dogs may help solve your problem! Truly, two beagles don't make much more work than one. Here again, the deciding factor may be whether you have enough space, money, and the like.

Male or Female?

How do we pick a puppy? Should it be a female or a male? If you have any thought of raising a litter some day, then the choice is already determined for you: You'll have to get a female. Of course, the breeding business involves males as well, but the owner of a male dog can only observe from a distance how the mother cares for the puppies.

If breeding isn't among your plans, you can consider either sex. Males generally grow up

TIP

Establishing Who's Boss

If you decide in favor of just one puppy, remember that it will consider you one of its own kind. Like other hunting hounds, the beagle is intelligent. You will have to deal with it sternly from the first day on, so that the young animal knows who is boss.

to be larger and tougher. My experience indicates that at some point, a male dog will test his power with you and see if he can boss you. A female seldom does this, although a female beagle is more likely to try it than a female dog of another breed.

In short, males are generally more independent and can be headstrong now and then. Also, males are more watchful. Don't be surprised, however, if your male beagle quickly warms up to a stranger. He may bark a few times, but then he will start wagging his tail and seem to say, "I don't know you, but I sure would like to be your friend!"

The independent spirit of beagle males can be real trouble, especially if a female in heat (*estrus*) is in the neighborhood. The odor pulls him irresistibly to the home of the female, where he may spend hours, even days. Generally, this goes along with a miserable-sounding mating call. This attracts other males, who join in the howling, which is hardly a pleasure for the owner of the female. Meanwhile, you have to do without the company of your beagle.

The situation doesn't have to degenerate to this point, however. If you have trained your

dog to respond to your call, you can call him back and suppress his wanderlust. Better yet, don't let your dog out of the house unless you have him on a leash.

It is easier to keep a female at home. Females have a yen to roam only when they are in heat, and most of them are in heat only twice a year, on the average. At that time, there will be some bloody discharge from her vagina for seven to ten days. You may want to get the right kind of sanitary napkin from the veterinarian, or you can make do by washing the bedding in the sleeping basket more frequently. If the discharge soils the carpet and furniture, you will have to get sanitary napkins.

While hormone injections have been given to control estrus in the past, the consensus today is that this treatment poses a danger of inflammation and infection, and should be avoided. The best way to deal with your dog's reproductive system is to eliminate it by spaying or neutering. Puppies are a big responsibility that should not be assumed by accident. If you are not actively planning to breed your pets, they should be spayed or neutered.

Space Considerations

Don't consider just yourself, consider your dog when you think about space. You want your dog to be happy. If you have a one-bedroom apartment on the tenth floor, you don't buy a Great Dane, Doberman pinscher, or German shepherd. I'm not just referring to physical space alone. Quality space is important too.

The ideal situation is to give your beagle a fenced-in yard. Still, if you live in an apartment, you can find ways to indulge your desire to keep a beagle. Basically, this means that you have to count on walking your dog at least an hour per day. On your days off, you will have to take it along to a park or the beach, where it can run off its almost boundless energy. Bored, sedentary beagles can become destructive.

The Dog Trade

You can't pick up a beagle just anywhere. You need to take some care. The best source is a reputable breeder. Adoption through a rescue group or humane society is an excellent alternative.

After you have determined the source of your puppy, be sure that you acquire the right paperwork, including pedigree and vaccinations. Buy with care and forethought. Don't buy on impulse.

Selecting a Breeder

If you decide to buy from a breeder, consult the experienced hands in your local beagle club and the representatives of the American Kennel Club. When you have found someone who seems good, take the trouble to confirm your selection.

Breeders who want only to sell puppies and show no interest in what you want to do with the puppy after you buy it are not the kind you should deal with. Expect the breeder to ask about the makeup of your family, your housing, and your plans. You may find that the breeder seems reluctant to sell if you live in a small apartment where it is hard to take walks every day.

Good breeders also take an interest in the quality of the puppy they sell you. They may ask you to take the animal to at least one dog

show, so that the breeder's success can be measured by the decision of an impartial judge.

Often, a discussion between buyer and seller leads to a genuinely friendly understanding. That's fine, provided that you don't lose sight of the business aspects of the relationship. You have the right to see the various papers, and the breeder has the obligation to show them to you. Some breeders do this with pleasure and undisguised pride. Others refuse, or look for an excuse. If that happens, get back into your car and take your business elsewhere.

A purebred beagle comes with a registration certificate from the American Kennel Club, or at least an application form. This form must be filled in properly and forwarded to the AKC (see page 90). There should also be a pedigree. The registration certificate is an official AKC document. If the breeder has already named the puppy you picked and has registered it, you must register the transfer and send the certificate with the appropriate fee to the AKC. The AKC then transfers the puppy to your ownership and keeps a record of it. You receive a new certificate. If the breeder gives you only an application for registration, you should complete it as quickly as possible, giving the name you selected for the puppy. Mail the completed

TIP

Worth Asking About

With your veterinarian's consent, you can give chlorophyll tablets to your female dog when she is in estrus. This will help to neutralize the scent of the female secretions that attract male dogs.

These two have become great friends!

application with the appropriate fee to the AKC headquarters in New York.

Understand that the pedigree is only a chart giving the puppy's ancestry. It is not a part of its official papers. Many breeders administer their own puppy vaccinations. Pups are then sold with a health/vaccination record, but not a veterinary certificate. Owners are then encouraged (or required by contract) to have their own veterinarian examine the puppy within three days or so of purchase to confirm freedom from health problems.

You would do well to plan to view your prospective puppy's litter several times. You may be excited about your future pet, but don't make a definite selection before the puppies are eight to nine weeks old. Breeders generally do not require you to select from a litter that is much younger.

Beagles are affectionate, even with other pets.

The beagle is one of the most popular show dogs in the United States.

Usually, business is done on a first come, first serve basis. You put your name on a waiting list, and your turn comes after the people whose names are higher on the list have had their turn. If your name tops the list, you have the choice of the litter. If you are, let's say, fourth on the list, then you can choose from all but the three puppies that have been sold or promised to another.

When the time comes, be sure you understand that you have the right to refuse to buy. The refusal can be based on a variety of circumstances. Perhaps the puppy doesn't appeal to you, or perhaps you've had another look around the kennel and things don't look right to you.

Your first visit should occur when the puppies are five to six weeks old. Your discussion with the breeder will tell you a lot. You should also pay attention to the female that mothered the litter and to other dogs on the premises. How do they act? Do they look well fed and well cared for? If they look good, the puppies are likely to be good. If the level of care is poor, then don't expect that the puppies will fare any better.

The puppies themselves should be the picture of health. By the time you make your choice, the eight- or nine-week-old puppies should be active and moving fairly fast. Sluggishness is a poor sign, unless the puppies have just finished a meal.

Selecting a Puppy

Good puppies should have meat on their frames, but their ribs should still be evident to the touch. Sunken flanks and protruding ribs point to poor feeding. Round bellies, which usually mean swollen bellies, mostly point to an infestation of intestinal worms; nowadays this is unacceptable for puppies of that age.

Pay close attention to the body openings. There should be no feces stuck under the tails, a sign of diarrhea. In female puppies, the area around the vagina should be clean, as should the foreskin of males. The drooping, low-set ears should also look clean.

There should be no pronounced odor beyond the natural puppy smell. Pay especially close attention to the eyes. They must be clean, wet, shiny, smooth, and transparent. Too much moisture in the eyes is also undesirable. Tears running down the cheeks are a sign of a possible infection, or worse.

Be sure to check inside the ears. A brown discharge in the ear canal indicates the presence of mites or infection.

If you pick the most adventurous puppy of the litter, you run a greater chance that it will try to dominate you—meaning that you may well have obedience problems. Don't pick the smallest puppy. It was probably held back in its development because of poor health. Perhaps you should consider which puppy's personality would be best suited to a particular home situation: for example, the more dominant puppy needs an adult situation where someone is prepared to administer strict discipline during training; the more settled personality is well suited to a family situation; and the rather submissive pup belongs in a quiet, secure home, perhaps with an elderly owner.

Finally, make sure that the puppy has a shiny coat and a nice color. I think that the tricolors are the most popular, but also attractive are the white with lemon or tan tigering, especially if they have a black nose and deep, dark eyes. Tan-and-white and lemon-and-white puppies are born almost completely white with a faint darker pattern like a jigsaw on the back and head. Tigering can be black marking on a blue ground, too. Other beagles are solid white, black, or orange.

As soon as you have made your selection, it is a good idea to tattoo your beagle puppy on the inner thigh. It is an even better idea to use an American Kennel Club registration number, since they will assist, when contacted (see addresses, page 90), in locating the dog's recorded owners.

However, there is no requirement that a dog be tattooed to be registered or shown or to participate in any other AKC activity.

Taking the Puppy Home

The best procedure is to arrange the transfer of your new puppy in advance. That way, the breeder can take precautions that minimize the chance of car sickness. Food should be withheld from the puppy or it should be fed lightly four hours before you plan to pick it up. If you insist on selecting a puppy and taking it with you on the spot, the risk is yours.

If it will be a long trip, take a thermos with water and a watering bowl.

Most reputable breeders will require the purchaser to bring along a safe traveling crate or container for the puppy to ride in. A puppy loose in your car is a major distraction and can become a flying object should you need to brake suddenly or become involved in an accident. Make sure that the container is large enough for the dog and that it provides adequate ventilation.

Furthermore, the dog should be kept away from the heat or air-conditioning vents. In the winter, the heated airflow can cause the dog to be overcome by heat. In the summer, the air-conditioning can cause stiff muscles.

Most dogs, including beagles, like to look out of the window during a car trip. That means they prefer sitting on a rear seat. For safety's sake, you can get at the pet store a canine seat belt that is designed specifically for dogs.

To train a new dog to ride in the back seat, take a passenger along for the first ride. That person can stroke the dog and talk to it encouragingly.

TIP

Kennel Precautions
If you are visiting more than one beagle breeder in the same day, be sure to wash your hands, either with soap and water or with antibacterial wipes. This will minimize the possibility of transmitting diseases from one kennel to another.

Some dogs keep having problems with car sickness. Your veterinarian has medicine for this condition, but it is healthier to get a dog gradually accustomed to riding in a car. Start during the first ride. Have your passenger keep a sharp eye on the puppy. If he or she notices any disquiet or salivation, stop the car immediately. Let the dog out for about ten minutes, and then resume the journey.

You may have to stop several times during the first ride, but don't let that get you down. The trouble you take then will pay off later. As soon as your new puppy is used to its new home, you can gradually expose it to more car trips. Start with a short, one-minute ride, then increase it to two, five, and more minutes. This way, most puppies quickly get used to riding in cars and don't get carsick.

Once you get your new puppy home safely, let it explore in an area where there is no danger from passing automobiles. Give it plenty of time to urinate or defecate before you take it inside. At that point, the puppy becomes part of the family and it will be totally dependent on you for its education, feeding, care, management, and housing.

Under good conditions, beagle puppies grow and develop quickly.

A crate often becomes the beagle's own special place in your home.

True to its nature, this pup is naturally inquisitive.

Beagles respond to anyone who pays attention to them.

HOW-TO: BASIC TRAINING

Housebreaking

All puppies need to be house-trained. This doesn't have to involve a big drama. Just count on spending a lot of time on the project for a week or two.

First, let the puppy out early each morning. Take it to the same spot, a section of lawn or whatever, where you will walk with it. You need to lead it, because it won't follow you on its own. This way, the puppy knows what you expect of it when you take it back to the same spot. In the beginning, you may have to take the puppy there every hour on the hour. At the very least, count on taking the puppy out after every meal and after every nap. There are also between-times when the puppy looks uneasy, sniffs, and walks in circles as if

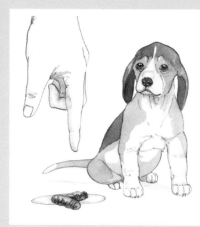

Oops? Make sure you get the "scent" of the dog's urine (not the droppings) on a piece of paper and place it on top of the other sheets. This will help your pet relocate the "right" area quickly.

searching for something. Until three to six months of age, bladder control is not yet fully established. Therefore, you must learn to be alert to your dog's needs and the physical signs it gives you.

You will find that your beagle puppy wants to keep its own sleeping area clean. This desire is usually instilled in a dog by its mother while she is nursing the litter. Once she no longer takes responsibility for cleaning up after each puppy's eliminations, the mother generally makes it quite clear that she wants elimination removed from the "den." The puppies learn quickly to comply, or suffer swift correction. Your job is to pick up where the mother left off.

Elimination should be handled with common sense. Until a puppy truly understands

what it is expected to do, accidents happen. These accidents are not evidence of willful misbehavior, so react swiftly, firmly, and fairly. To show your displeasure, "no" should suffice. Then give the puppy a clear indication of the proper procedure.

Take the dog to the elimination area and praise it. Correction should only be attempted if you actually catch the puppy in the process of relieving itself. Clean each "accident" site to remove urine odor and avoid reattracting the dog to the spot. Use soapy water and a little vinegar or a special solution available at pet stores. Don't use household ammonia, which will only enhance the problem. (Ammonia in the urine attracts the dog to the spot in the first place.)

Never forget to praise your puppy for its successful efforts. Lavish stroking, verbal praise, and hugs can be more effective than edible rewards.

Paper Training

If it is not convenient to train your puppy to eliminate outdoors, you may wish to use paper training as a temporary measure. In this case, use the urine scent as an aid by saving a soaked wad to remind your pet where the correct spot is.

Start by spreading a large area with newspaper—a small room with a linoleum or tile floor is ideal. Then, gradually reduce the area that is covered with paper; but be certain to leave a urine-soaked portion behind whenever you replace the paper. In time, you should be able to reduce the "correct" spot to a square yard (m) or so.

Crates

You need to take special precautions for the night. Dogs sleep enough during the day that they have energy left at night for taking a walk through the house. You can let older dogs do this without worry, but you need to guard against a puppy's making a puddle or pile somewhere in the house. You do this by shutting the puppy in a confined area—a small, uncarpeted room, a special cage, or a roomy crate. Suitable crates can be purchased in a pet shop. Don't make the mistake of thinking of the crate as a prison. Your beagle will probably accept it as a den—and a den is something to be kept clean. Don't place water or food bowls inside the crate.

Before you, yourself, turn in, take the dog for a last walk and then put it in the crate. Secure the door, and then you can go to sleep.

Maybe not for long! Puppies are used to having their mother and littermates around from the day they were born. They are used to the body heat put out by their family, which isn't available to them now. To keep the puppy warm in its box, put a hot water bottle inside it. If the bottle is quite warm, protect the puppy by wrapping an old blanket around the hot water bottle.

A puppy relies heavily on its sense of smell to locate the area where it is to relieve itself.

The puppy is also used to nocturnal sounds made by its dam and littermates. By contrast, your house may be quite silent once everyone has retired. You'll have to do something about that, too. A good method is to put a ticking clock outside the box. That accustoms the puppy to a monotonous, reassuring sound. Some dog fanciers say that the sound of the alarm clock is something like the beat of the mother dog's heart—a sound that the puppy has long been used to.

Place a few old blankets in the crate, so the puppy can bed down on something soft. With all that, you will have prepared the puppy for a good, restful night.

Still, many puppies seem to have trouble falling asleep the first few nights. They whine constantly and keep the whole household awake. If this occurs, you may try speaking reassuringly to the puppy. Whether or not this works, be prepared to persevere. It doesn't take all that long to break in a new puppy. After three or four days, it will probably sleep quietly all night long.

BASIC RULES OF BEAGLE CARE

You will probably have a dog bed ready for your new puppy, but before you introduce it there, let it become acquainted with the entire layout of your home.

Getting the Puppy Settled

Everything is new to the puppy, and it will want to investigate everything with its nose and eyes. It has no time for anything else! Several hours may pass before it decides to look for a place to take a short rest. Soon it will be sniffing around again. Don't be surprised if the puppy's resting place is right in front of your feet. Especially during the first two days, the puppy will want to stay in your immediate vicinity.

The intensive sniffing can take several days, because, as I mentioned, the beagle puppy is a hunting hound. After four or five days, however, the puppy behaves as if it has lived with you for years. It knows all corners and openings and is especially familiar with places where it can look out of a window without losing its balance.

With good care, a beagle will flourish, and be a joy to own.

Those first few days, be sure to follow the feeding schedule and menu established by the breeder. If you want to change the diet, don't change it abruptly. Do it gradually over a period of several days to avoid diarrhea.

A Private Spot

If you decide not to use a crate, your beagle will still need a private spot in your house to which you can send it when you don't want it underfoot and where it can spend the night. Dogs don't have a preference for any particular spot. They accept the space you assign them. You can't, however, keep changing the dog's spot in the house. Dogs are creatures of habit and don't follow if you move their space from here to there.

Choosing a location: There are varied opinions about the best location. People have used a large, well-ventilated kitchen closet, a corner in the den, or the space between two pieces of furniture, like a bookcase and a bench. Any of these is all right with the beagle, as long as it can be close to its human friends. It wouldn't like a space in a room that people don't use much.

The most important consideration is that the dog's crate or private spot be free of drafts and moisture. Further, the spot should be easy to clean, so provide a removable liner. However, this liner should not be too hard, because this would promote calluses. You need to protect the dog's pressure points, which are the hock joints, the elbows, and the pasterns. An old blanket is ideal.

Don't put the dog's space too close to a stove or heat outlet. I know of a beagle that had almost constant problems with an earache because it had the habit of lying on the grate of the central heating system. Set it up so the dog will be comfortably warm but not so hot that the difference between inside and outside temperatures is excessive. Bear in mind that dogs generally prefer cooler temperatures than do human beings.

Choosing furniture: Furniture for the dog's spot can be varied. You can use a dog bed, of which there are a variety on the market. Put a few blankets inside, and it makes a fine resting place.

Dog beds are typically made of heavy fabric or fleece that covers an insert stuffed with polyfil or cedar.

Also popular are the snuggle ball-type beds, which look similar to a bean-bag chair and allow the beagle to create a more body-hugging nest.

The Doghouse

You may decide to house the beagle outdoors in its own doghouse. A reason for this decision could be lack of space inside your home or a desire to keep the beagle from constantly being underfoot.

I see no objection to a doghouse, provided you can protect your beagle from moisture, drafts, and cold. Cold should not be a serious concern. Beagles can stand relatively low temperatures because they grow a new, thick coat of fur in the fall. You should, however, do everything you can to keep dogs warm at all times.

Doghouse Construction

The floor should be at least 1¼ inch (3 cm) thick. Raise it off the ground at least 4 inches (10 cm) with wooden props to permit proper ventilation.

To get the right dimensions for the doghouse, measure your beagle. The two measurements you need most are height at the withers (the high point of the shoulders) and length, measured between the base of the tail and the withers.

The height of the doghouse should be at least one-and-a-half times the height of your beagle at the withers. The depth should be at least one-and-a-half times your dog's length.

Along one side of the doghouse, build a corridor that runs the length of the house. At the back, make a doorway from the corridor into the rest of the house; make the doorway as wide as the corridor. The rest of the doghouse is the beagle's sleeping quarters, which will measure one "dog height" by one-and-one-half "dog lengths."

Make the front of the house higher than the rear, so water can run off the roof. Let the roof project over the front of the house by about 8 inches (20 cm) or more. At the sides and the rear, it should project at least 2 inches (5 cm). The roof must be moisture proof. Make it removable for easier cleaning of the doghouse.

Feel free to make the floor space of the house larger if you like. You must certainly do this if the house should hold more than one beagle.

If you like, you can also build a window into the front of the house. Remember, however, that most dogs look out by pressing their snouts against the glass, so that the window quickly becomes dirty.

I suggest you get a self-closing door for the doghouse, which you can buy in a pet store. The door is easy to install and helps keep the house free from drafts. Cover the floor with old blankets, sheets, or the like.

The Run

To build a run, provide floor space of at least 24 square feet (7 m^2); the width should be about 1 yard (approximately 1 m) or more. Beagles can move freely inside this space, but there's nothing wrong with providing additional room.

Be sure the floor isn't moist. You have a choice of several floorings: gravel, dry sand, a grass mat, tile, or concrete. However, the flooring must be cleansed and disinfected, so it is best to choose a substance that is impervious to water.

At least one of the sides of the run should be made of chain-link fencing with a mesh size of 2 inches (5 cm). A trellis is all right, but it is more difficult to construct. You can build a kennel in the space between three walls, but it's more pleasant for the dog to have a free run.

The run should be connected to the doghouse. Don't make the doghouse smaller, though, because of the run.

Boarding Kennels

When you go on vacation without your beagle, you must plan ahead. You can leave the dog with family, friends, or neighbors or ask someone to dog-sit. If that doesn't work, you must find a boarding kennel. Not all of these are equally good, so get a recommendation from fellow members of the beagle club or from your veterinarians, who may even operate a kennel themselves.

TIP

The Happy Observer

If you want to make your beagle really happy, give it a spot up off the floor, where it can see more of the activity around it. Provide space on a bench or an old chair. An old reclining chair is ideal. You can cover it with an old blanket, or you can get one of the modern polyester blankets that look like lamb's fleece. These are simple to launder.

Good kennels are booked early, so count on making reservations for your dog before you make reservations for your own trip. You may have to book space for your dog in November or December if you want to go on vacation in July or August.

Reputable kennels insist that your beagle's vaccinations be current. Check with the kennel about what vaccinations are required and with your veterinarian to be sure the vaccinations you have are current. Also be sure your dog is free of fleas and other parasites.

Beagles love to romp and play, and eagerly explore every nook and cranny.

When you take your beagle to the kennel, ask the person in charge if you may take along a dog bed or another familiar piece of furniture. Toys and other equipment of that type are better left at home.

Check ahead to see what type of feed they use at the kennel. You may even want to take along a good supply of your beagle's favorite food if you think there may be any trouble with eating.

Even so, your beagle may eat little or nothing while it is at the kennel. Beagles are devoted pets and they easily become homesick. Your dog may look starved, wild, and nervous when you see it again. Don't blame the kennel operator. If you selected the kennel wisely, the operator will have done the best possible under the circumstances.

In any event, inspect your pet for fleas and flea dirt before returning from the kennel to avoid infesting your home.

TIP

Sun vs. Shade

Pay attention to the direction of the sun. Beagles love to sunbathe, preferably on a raised platform. When it gets too hot, however, they seek protection in the shade. You should position the run so that the beagle can find both sun and shade.

Beagles like to investigate all sorts of containers.

The beagle is generally amiable but it can also be extremely headstrong.

Traveling with Your Beagle

If your dog goes along on vacation, make sure that the hotels and motels you book accept dogs (see page 90 and phone in advance). Take along a folding kennel. This is constructed so that it can fit into a small space, and you'll be able to put it into your car.

Some states and most foreign countries require vaccination before they allow your dog to enter. Some even require a quarantine, in which case you'd better not plan to take your dog. Be sure to get this type of information ahead of time. Call your veterinarian, your travel agent, or the consulate of the country you plan to visit.

Take along your beagle's regular feeding dishes, dog bed, blanket, collar and leash, comb and brush, and a first-aid kit. Make sure you'll be able to get your dog's familiar food en route. Check with the travel agent in case of doubt. If the agent doesn't know, write to the manufacturer of the product you use.

The Security Room

There will doubtlessly be times when a young or adult beagle must stay at home alone. It may happen every day. Therefore, you should train your beagle from the first day to be locked into a secure room where it can't do too much damage and where it will not injure itself. The first day, put the dog into the security room along with a familiar dog bed and toys. Start with about ten minutes of solitude, and keep quiet during that time. If your beagle thinks you're around, it will spend all its energy to get to you as quickly as possible. Lengthen the time of solitude by several minutes on successive days until the dog can remain quiet for an entire hour.

The first few days you'll hear howls and cries, but if you make confinement a regular thing, your beagle will accept it, not as a punishment, but as a regular part of the daily routine. It will learn to amuse itself if you provide a hard rubber ball or a nylon bone.

Of course, don't leave a rug or carpet in the security room. The flooring should be tile or wood, so that you can easily clean feces and urine. If there are curtains, be sure they are high off the ground, so the dog can't reach them. Also, don't keep a bookcase with books in the room, because beagles love to play with and tear at books and magazines. I learned that lesson from bitter experience!

Toys—Good and Bad

It pays to buy proper toys for your beagle. Veterinarians tell endless stories about strange objects they have removed from the stomachs of dogs, including stones, balls, needles, nails, corks, and rubber bands. As you may suspect, some of these objects can cause all sorts of damage.

A Baby's Arrival

If you expect a new baby, give your beagle extra attention so that it doesn't feel its position in the family is threatened. When the baby comes, let the beagle be with you when you tend the child. Let the beagle smell the baby, and meanwhile speak to the dog gently and kindly. Try to avoid ordering the beagle away when you're with the baby. This just makes the beagle insecure about the "intruder" in the family.

Dogs don't swallow objects because they're hungry. They do it in the course of play. You can avoid this problem by furnishing entertaining and safe toys. Many beagles love to play with a ball, but make it a proper ball. Small balls, like Ping-Pong balls and marbles, are not recommended because they can be swallowed and choke the dog. Don't get a ball that your beagle can bite through, and don't get one that doesn't bounce.

Squeaking toys are also not recommended. Even if the squeaking doesn't drive you crazy, they can be dangerous. Your beagle can quickly gnaw apart the toy so that the squeaker drops out, and in nine out of ten cases the beagle will swallow it. Surgery is generally the only solution!

Many synthetic materials are dangerous, as are toys made of wood that splinters easily. Rubber balls and rubber bones are suitable only if your beagle just plays with them. If it starts biting and chewing on them, take them away. Rubber is not digestible and can cause intestinal upsets.

Imitation bones made of rawhide and similar toys are ideal, as are artificial bones, balls, and rings of hard nylon (but don't get those coated with chocolate).

Beagles and Children

Beagles are affectionate and adore children. They are wonderful companions, gentle, playful, and even-tempered. In fact, beagles are also friendly to other pets, including other dogs and even cats. I once knew a beagle that daily licked clean the ears of a cat in the household; the cat, in turn, groomed the beagle!

TIP

Toy Tips

I recommend that you give proper toys to puppies when they are quite young. Toys strengthen their teeth and exercise their chewing muscles.

An old shoe has been used as a dog toy for ages, but I don't recommend it. Tanned leather doesn't dissolve well in the stomach, and if your beagle swallows pieces of any size, they can cause blockage of the intestines. Further, you are setting up a potentially confusing situation, since your puppy will not understand the difference between an old slipper and your brand-new one! I advise against letting your beagle play with leather shoes and slippers.

On the other hand, beagles are spirited dogs, and if they get into conflict with a child, the child may not be able to hold its own. Beagles love to play with children and may even take the role of protector; this doesn't mean that children can treat beagles any way they like. Teach your children not to abuse or threaten your family pet. Also, teach them to recognize when the beagle wants to be left alone and when it invites play. Beagles often make such invitations, but there are moments when they really want to be alone and left in peace.

For that reason, it's important for you to keep an eye on the situation when a beagle and a child play together. My point is this: Be sure to teach your children to treat your dog properly.

top left: Beagles love being outside in the fresh air.

top right: Beagles often become very attached to particular members of the family. They are excellent with children.

left: Beagles get along well together and arguments are rare.

top left: All beagles play with boundless energy. Everything interests them.

top right: Don't these two adorable beagle puppies look cute enough for a picture postcard?

right: Many beagles become extremely attached to their first toys.

When you acquire a beagle, you may be tempted by all the fancy equipment offered in the pet store. Think through your needs calmly, and buy only what you find useful. Here is a list of helpful or necessary items.

✔ A lined leather or soft nylon collar is useful, especially if your puppy is a bit wild. In fact, I recommend a harness for such cases.

✔ A leash of normal length—about 6 feet (2 m)—is good to use when you take the beagle for a walk. Since puppies love to gnaw at anything resembling leather, consider getting a leash with a short section of chain links at the end. At any rate, do what you can to keep the puppy from gnawing on the leash; it's not good for the dog.

✔ Also get a long or reel leash, the kind with a spring that automatically rolls up. It helps your dog let off extra energy when you go for a walk, and it is also very handy for training purposes.

✔ Get two dishes, one for food and one for water. Since beagles are lop-eared, get dishes that narrow toward the top. Get heavy models that can't be upset or pushed away easily. You can minimize having dishes pushed around too much by gluing a strip of rubber on the bottom.

✔ A metal comb and a brush are also important (see page 39). Also get a narrow-toothed "louse comb." Use brushes with natural bristles. I also recommend a grooming glove.

✔ Get tweezers and a good brand of flea powder.

✔ Get no-rinse shampoo at your pet store. This can serve as a waterless bath. It is often used for show dogs which may require more frequent touch-up cleaning. It will also provide protection against fleas and other pests. I personally like to use it when the beagles are still quite small.

✔ A protective spray for the paws can come in quite handy, especially if you take your beagle for a walk in the woods in winter, with snow on the ground. The spray protects against road salts, and it keeps the pads from becoming cracked and sore.

✔ To keep away all types of vermin such as fleas, mites and ticks, apply monthly

The long or reel leash enables you to adjust the free play when walking your beagle.

EQUIPMENT

Biospot or Onespot-type products. A few drops should be administered topically behind the dogs' shoulders. These products are the safest and most effective means of flea control for a smooth-coat breed such as the beagle. Flea collars and powders are no longer the preferred method of treating for these parasites, and a number of bloodlines are hereditarily predisposed to having adverse, allergic reactions to these products.

✔ A repellent spray is a good defense when young puppies forget their toilet training. The spray can help wipe out the dirty traces of misplaced feces or urine. To prevent more damage, you can spray in house corners and entryways and on furniture, carpet, certain trees and bushes, and flowers, among other places.

✔ Also important are protective panties made of heavy material to put on a female in

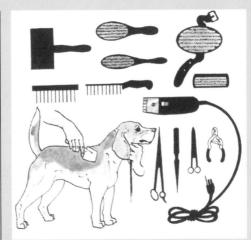

Daily grooming is important for your beagle. You should use a narrow-toothed comb and a brush with natural bristles. After a thorough combing— with the lay of the fur—the beagle should be brushed just as thoroughly.

heat; they are available in any pet store. This keeps your carpet, furniture, and other household goods from becoming soiled. They come in different sizes; ask your veterinarian for advice.

✔ Rubber massage brushes and/or rubber grooming gloves are essential for grooming your short-haired beagle.

✔ Get a metal identification tag, either one that hangs from an "S" hook or one that lies flat against the collar. Leather pockets, attached to the collar as a means of identification, are outdated. These metal tags should be engraved or stamped with the name of the owner and have further contact information.

Dog bowls come in many shapes and sizes. Dishes that are narrow at the top are best for beagles.

GROOMING

It's no surprise that a well-groomed beagle is a healthy, contented dog. But grooming involves more than just coat care.

Care of the Teeth

A few weeks after whelping, puppies get their baby teeth. Several months later, these are exchanged for permanent teeth. Generally this causes no problems, but in a rare case, the eyeteeth (canine teeth) don't drop out. You'll notice sharp, pointed baby teeth next to or behind the permanent eyeteeth. The baby teeth must be removed, or they will push the permanent teeth from their place. Take your young beagle to the veterinarian and have the old eyeteeth removed if they persist beyond the ninth month of life.

Generally, you needn't expect trouble with teeth until your beagle reaches one-and-a-half to two years of age. After that, you may start noticing plaque, a soft deposit formed by decaying food, bacteria, and saliva. At first it is rather white, but soon the color changes to yellow. Most plaque starts at the gum line, then spreads over the enamel of the tooth.

A well-groomed beagle requires considerable care, but the result is very rewarding.

If not removed, plaque may create cornice-like extensions overhanging adjacent teeth but not actually covering them.

Plaque is easy to remove. Brush the teeth from time to time, and the plaque disappears. You should use a regular toothbrush and a special meat-flavored toothpaste, available from your pet store or veterinarian. Don't use an abrasive tooth cleanser. This removes the plaque all right, but also causes slight damage to the enamel.

Your beagle needs to learn at a young age that its teeth are going to be brushed at times. If you don't get it accustomed to this procedure, you'll always have your hands full trying to get the dog to sit still and keep its mouth open.

Don't worry too much about caries (cavities). They don't often occur in dogs.

Foot Care

Many dogs have a lot of hair growing between the toes, although this is a lesser problem in beagles. Still, check your beagle to make sure that hair growth there isn't excessive because this can make dogs quite uncomfortable. The toes are bent apart, and the usual, beautiful, round, closed foot becomes a splay-foot, interfering with walking and standing. So keep an eye on those hairs between the toes and clip them if necessary. Don't go so far as to shave them off completely because a certain amount of hair is good protection for the skin.

Also check for hair between the foot pads. This hair can also cause problems—for instance if the dog steps into a discarded piece of chewing gum. When the gum sticks to objects as the dog walks and pulls on the hair, the dog is in pain. You can prevent this whole scenario by keeping the pad hairs short. This also helps prevent trouble in the winter, when snow and ice can stick to the pad hairs, making the foot a clump of ice. So keep a sharp eye on your dog's pads in freezing weather.

Your dog can get sore pads from small cracks that develop there. As long as the cracks stay shallow, they should be considered normal, but if they become deep, you must take action. You don't want your dog to limp or go lame. Start by rubbing the pads with a good baby salve, cod-liver oil salve, or any salve with a glycerine base. If this doesn't bring relief in a day or two, consult a veterinarian. In any case, I suggest you put booties on the sore feet (available at your local pet store) to keep the pad free from dirt until the wounds have healed. Booties will also come in handy for winter walks, particularly on salted city sidewalks and streets.

Care of the Nails

Beagles that walk on hard surfaces keep wearing down their nails so that they never need to be cut. If you keep your beagle on soft surfaces or don't let it exercise much, the nails tend to grow too long.

Nail clipping isn't hard, particularly if you train your beagle to tolerate it at an early age. Take a strong pair of clippers—available commercially in several models—and trim a piece of the nail. It's very simple.

Just don't clip too deeply. The nail grows around a tiny cone of connective tissue that contains blood vessels and nerves. When you cut too deeply, you clip off the tip of this sensitive tissue. The dog will jump up in pain, and blood may spurt from the wound. Naturally, your dog will never again sit still for another nail clipping.

The lesson is clear: Never clip into the live part of the nail. If the nails are white and transparent, it is generally easy to see where the live part starts. Tissue with capillaries shows with a bluish tinge. But if the nails are black or dark, you won't be able to see these signs and you will have to use your good judgment. Some people quickly develop a sense of where to cut and seldom make a mistake. Others err repeatedly.

I advise that you cut only up to the point where the cut nail is just above the ground when the dog stands upright normally. Then you can round off the cut end neatly with a file so that there are no rough edges.

If you do tap blood, let the wound bleed for a little while. Then apply styptic powder or press the wound closed with a bandage. When the bleeding stops, put some nonstinging iodine on the wound. If you don't trust yourself to do the nail trimming right, let a professional do it for you.

There is one instance in which you shouldn't hesitate to take prompt action yourself; that is when your beagle just about tears out a nail during a fast run or rough play. If you don't attend to a loose nail, it will cause your beagle recurring pain and trouble. So take the loose nail tightly in your fingers and pull it out with a quick motion. Treat it with a disinfecting wound powder, then cover the wound with a clean, sterile piece of surgical gauze. When the wound is completely dry, you can let the dog go.

A torn nail is quite painful, and you may not be able to clean it adequately without sedation. Antibiotics may also be required to prevent infection. It is wise, therefore, to consult your veterinarian after administering the first aid described above.

If the nail is completely torn out, it does not grow back, although a short stump may develop. You can file this down from time to time to keep it nice and round. This job is really simple.

Dewclaws will require regular trimming. If not cut back regularly, they can become snagged, or grow in a full circle, causing the hound a lot of discomfort.

The Ears

Beagles and many other hunting hounds have hanging or "flap ears" that protect the ear canal against dust and dirt. This is an advantage in the hunt, when dogs have to chase after prey across dusty and muddy terrain. However, the long flaps also require some special attention.

Care of the Flaps

The ear flaps should be washed from time to time, perhaps during an overall bath. It is

amazing how much dirt can accumulate along the edges. This dirt is a mixture of wax, dust, sand, and hairs. If soap and water don't get rid of it, use cotton balls or swabs moistened with a little rubbing alcohol. Be very gentle. Also, be aware that this treatment removes all body fats. So follow it up with an application of baby oil.

A problem can arise if a beagle comes down with an ear infection that causes it to scratch its ears hard or shake them against a chair, table leg, wall, or cupboard. This can cause subcutaneous bleeding (an ear flap hematoma), which needs to be relieved by the veterinarian—an operation that is not at all simple. Naturally, prevention is better than having to cure. If you see your beagle shake its ears against the furniture, take a close look and be sure the dog doesn't have an ear infection.

Hair in the Ear Canal

The ear canal is lined with skin that can grow hair, particularly near the opening. Some breeds are especially hairy and experience frequent problems with hair in the ears. This is not the case with beagles, but I still recommend checking the ear occasionally. Too much hair can keep the ear canal from being properly ventilated, which can foster infections.

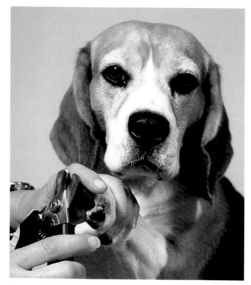

Get your beagle used to having its teeth brushed.

Several types of clippers are available. The guillotine-type works well.

The body of the beagle should be compact, not too short, and not too long—but in proportion.

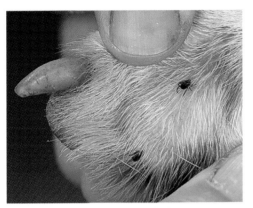

Upon its return from a wooded or grassy area, always inspect your beagle for ticks, including its feet.

Beagles are natural fielders and hunters. No wonder junior is very observant.

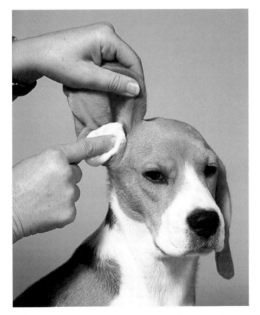

Clean the ear with a cotton swab. Do not probe into the ear canal. Clean only the external parts of the ear and the ear flap. Hold your pet's head firmly.

When bathing your beagle, use a shampoo specially formulated for short-haired dogs.

If you see too much hair growth, pull it out carefully with a pair of tweezers. Beagles don't like people messing with their ears, so do the job with kindness and gentleness. Once again, train your dog to tolerate the process while it is still quite young.

Cleaning the Ear Canal

If your beagle is healthy and its ear is functioning properly, you never (or hardly ever) have to clean out the ear canal. It tends to be self-cleaning. You should still inspect the canal, however.

Start by checking if there is ear wax and, if so, how much. Notice the color. If it is light to dark brown, all is well. Use your sense of smell. If there's a stench, suspect an ear infection. Rub the base of the ear directly behind the juncture with the head. If you hear "sloshing," there is an excess of exudates and perhaps an infection. At the least indication of an ear infection, immediately consult your veterinarian. If you are sure that nothing serious is wrong, continue cleaning the ears. Use an otic solution, which you can obtain from your veterinarian.

Ear Mites

A type of mite (Otodectes cynotis) lives in the dog's ear canal. This ear mite causes an ear infection, which can be detected by excessive wax that is generally reddish brown to black in color. The consistency of the wax generally turns grainy. The infection itches and causes the dog to scratch. As the infection progresses, your beagle will be in pain. It will hold its head at an angle and shake its ears. Depend on your veterinarian to get rid of this pest.

Fleas

Dog fleas are 0.08 to 0.12 inch (2–3 mm) in size, with the females somewhat larger than the males. They are reddish brown and have six legs.

Fleas mainly infest the neck, the back, the legs, and the base of the tail. They bite the dog, causing an itch. The dog reacts by scratching, biting, and chafing at the itch. A heavy infestation can greatly weaken the dog. It becomes thin and suffers from anemia. Young dogs can even die from a bad infestation. Furthermore, fleas can serve as intermediate hosts for tapeworms.

Don't delay treatment. As soon as you notice fleas, wash your beagle thoroughly with an anti-parasitic shampoo. Then consult with your veterinarian for the safest and most effective monthly treatment.

Flea larvae are quite sensitive to moisture, so it helps to scrub the house thoroughly with an insecticide dissolved in water. Pay close attention to cracks and seams in the floor and to wall-to-wall carpets.

If the dog continues to scratch itself, look for another cause. Perhaps there is something in the feed that causes a skin irritation.

Lice

Lice rarely occur on beagles, but if present the veterinarian should be consulted before attempting home treatments; a special shampoo for lice is the usual method of eliminating them, but special care should be taken to prevent overdosing your beagle with toxins. All flea and lice treatments, along with worming, are basically poisons; their use should be carefully timed to avoid undue stress on your puppy's systems.

Ticks

Ticks are arachnids. Males are about 0.06 to 0.08 inch (1½–2 mm) long and reddish brown or black in color. Females are 0.16 inch (4 mm) long and yellowish red.

Ticks hide in low bushes. When a beagle walks by, they drop down, especially during the summer months. They attach themselves to the skin and suck blood. In a few days, the body of the tick grows to the size of a pea and becomes bluish gray.

Keep an eye open for ticks when you stroke your beagle and when you groom it, which you ought to do daily, especially in summer.

A tick clamps its mouthpiece into the skin of the dog and is therefore difficult to remove. If you try to pull off the tick, the head of the tick remains and can quickly cause an infection that is quite painful to the dog. The best way to remove a tick is to use alcohol or acetone. Place one drop on the tick's head. Wait a moment, and then you can lift the pest from the dog's skin with a pair of tweezers. Do not twist. Use firm and constant upward pressure. Disinfect the place where the tick was attached. Then, drop the tick into a saucer of alcohol and leave it there for several hours, or simply flush it down the toilet.

Rocky Mountain spotted fever: Dog ticks can transmit Rocky Mountain spotted fever (Borelliosis)—a dangerous disease characterized by muscular pains, high fever, and skin eruptions. Since the disease is endemic throughout North America, anyone who comes in contact with animals and displays these symptoms should see a physician immediately.

Lyme disease: Beagles of any age can contract Lyme disease from a deer tick. This is a serious, potentially fatal illness. If you notice swelling and signs of tenderness around your pet's joints, contact your veterinarian. Should you find a tick on your beagle or suspect that it has been bitten, consultation is always recommended. If you have been bitten, see your physician immediately. With Lyme disease, timely diagnosis and treatment are essential.

Wouldn't you just want to take this pair of beagle puppies home with you?

Beagles are known to roam and often get lost. Be sure they always carry identification.

HOW-TO: COAT CARE

Washing

Beagles have a different concept of cleanliness than you do. They may lick parts of their bodies from time to time, but they don't go much further in taking care of themselves. As a result, you will have to turn your hand to grooming. Basically, you need to brush the dog regularly, comb it, and wash it now and then.

Dogs secrete sebum, a type of natural lubricant that keeps the hair and skin supple. When you wash your beagle, the sebum is dissolved and rinsed away. Since the sebum will soon return, no harm is done. Nevertheless, it is best not to wash the beagle at all until there is a good reason for it.

A good time for a bath is when your pet decides to take a mud bath, rolls in rotting leaves, or gets manure on its fur. You don't want to get dirt and stench in the house, so a bath is the only solution. You can also wash the dog if it is shedding. If you use a lot of water, comfortably hot, you'll help loosen the hairs. Then, when you brush the beagle while the fur dries, you'll brush out most of the hair, shortening the shedding time.

Use only a shampoo made especially for short-haired dogs. You'll find many good brands at the pet store that remove a minimum amount of sebum from the hair. If your beagle has problems with its coat, ask your veterinarian for a medicated shampoo that can help. Many dog shampoos contain an insecticide that removes fleas, ticks, and other vermin during the bath.

Generally, beagles like the bath. They enjoy swimming, after all. Some beagles hate getting water in their ear canal, however. You'll get a hint of this if you see the dog constantly shake its head. So put a good wad of cotton balls in the ears before you start.

Then wet the dog's whole body with lukewarm water. The best place to work is on a rubber mat in the bathtub. When the beagle is wet all over, massage some shampoo through the hairs and onto the skin. Take your time, so that the shampoo penetrates as deeply as possible. Then, thoroughly rinse away the shampoo. Then, shampoo a second

Active dogs, like the beagle, should have a regular bath. Be sure not to get any water or shampoo in your beagle's ears and eyes.

time. As you rub it in, you'll probably get a good foam, which helps the shampoo penetrate even better. Really take your time with the second round, especially if there is an insecticide in the shampoo. To be effective against fleas and other vermin, the shampoo has to stay on the dog at least ten minutes. Again rinse—thoroughly. Don't skimp on water. You don't want to leave shampoo on your beagle. If shampoo dries on the fur, it can cause the hair to rub off, causing a skin irritation or infection.

When bathing for fleas, start on neck and head and proceed toward paws and tail to avoid driving the fleas toward the eyes and ears.

Now take the cotton out of the ears and dry the dog. You can use an ordinary hand-held blow dryer. Be sure to brush the coat while you dry it. Brush lightly in the direction in which the hairs grow so that the hair drops down smoothly and doesn't become matted. (Matting isn't usually a problem with beagles.) Brush one area of coat at a time. When you've covered the whole dog, go over the fur with a comb to detect any small remaining snarls. Loosen these carefully.

Brushing

Generally, your beagle requires a bath only once or twice a year, but a good brushing is a frequent requirement. After a few sessions, your beagle will be used to it; it will pull back its hind legs and lie like a prince while it enjoys the grooming. Don't be fooled because your beagle's coat generally looks neat; a brushing is absolutely necessary. It helps remove any loose hair.

Grooming your pet with a brush while it is under the hair dryer massages the skin and loosens bits of scale.

You can obtain a special rubber brush made for short-haired dogs. Pull this through the fur several times, and you'll collect a good number of loose hairs. Brushing also massages the skin, loosening scaly skin. The scales work their way through the hair and rest on top of the coat, making it look dusty. Just leave the dusty scales there. In a half-hour's time, the dog will have shaken off a good many of them. After that, remove the rest with a damp washcloth. If you want to do a really professional job, use a grooming glove or a chamois cloth.

Always brush from the neck across the back to the tail in strong strokes. Then brush from the neck across the shoulders and along the front legs, downward, and again from the neck along the flanks, across the hip, and downward along the rear legs.

THE PROPER DIET

Foods for dogs can be split into two groups: those of animal origin and those of plant origin. The latter, which only indirectly forms part of the dog's diet in nature, leaves the digestive system largely unused if not suitably processed.

Meat

Some people believe that since dogs are carnivores, they should be fed only meat. That's an oversimplification, and it ignores advances in modern nutrition. The modern concept is based on the body's need for protein, carbohydrates, fat, vitamins, and minerals.

Meat is rich in protein and fat, both of which can also be found in foods of plant origin. However, meat is low or lacking in certain of the other basic nutritional elements. So, we have to add sources of carbohydrate to the diet, as well as some essential minerals and vitamins.

There are two main categories of protein: animal and vegetable. Animal proteins have a greater nutritional value than plant proteins. The most important sources of animal protein are meat (beef, mutton, goat, poultry, veal, fish), milk, eggs (probably the best available source of protein!), and fresh cheese (recommended

Only the best is good enough! Provide high-quality dog food for your pet.

mainly when your pet is eating poorly or is recovering from illness).

Other Protein Sources

Fish (although sometimes allergenic to dogs) is an excellent source of protein. It carries a higher biologic rating than red meat (at least a value of 80) and is also a good source of unsaturated fat. Always boil freshwater fish to inactivate an element that would otherwise destroy vitamin B_1. Don't feed smoked and salted fish. Naturally, be on guard against bones; they should be carefully removed from your beagle's rations.

I particularly recommend *hake* (dried cod), which contains 71 percent protein. It is strengthening and nourishing if fed occasionally, and it is convenient, as it can be handled dry. So is *fish meal*, which is prepared commercially in the same way as animal meal.

Milk is a well-balanced source of calcium and phosphorus, but cow's milk is lower in protein and fat than bitch's milk.

Cow's milk is also high in lactose (milk sugar), which many dogs have difficulty digesting. The issue is whether the dog produces enough of the enzyme lactase, which digests milk lactose. As the dog ages, it tends to produce less lactase. If you run into problems with diarrhea, feed less milk or replace it with buttermilk, which is also very healthy for dogs.

Eggs are probably the best available source of protein. The biologic rating of chicken eggs, for example, is a high 96. Always boil eggs for three minutes or so, to inactivate avidin and antitrypsin. Avidin counteracts biotin, and antitrypsin counteracts trypsin, a digestive enzyme.

Eggs are especially important for young dogs, and even an older dog can make use of an occasional egg in the diet for extra strength. However, eggs are allergenic, and too many eggs can increase the risk of arteriosclerosis in dogs, just as in humans. Soft-boiled eggs are excellent to keep stud dogs in prime breeding condition. Eggs also serve to strengthen dogs weakened by sickness or dogs with a poor coat.

Cheese provides a good source of protein and fat, but it should be fed to dogs only if prepared from milk without additives. Feed only fresh cheese, and be sure to remove any plastic rind. Never feed moldy cheese.

Cheese, which may also be allergenic in dogs, is recommended mainly when your pet is eating poorly or is recovering from illness.

Carbohydrates

Dogs depend principally on foods of vegetable origin for their carbohydrates. However, the dog's natural digestive organs can't break down the cell walls of plants, so that unprocessed vegetables, grains, and the like are almost indigestible. They must be adapted to your beagle's needs by chopping, grinding, and cooking.

Grains are indigestible for dogs as whole grain. The food value inside the grains must be released by processing. When ground into flour, they become quite digestible, however, and grains like corn are often used in commercial dog food. A number of other products furnish digestible grains.

Bread, contrary to popular belief, may be fed to your beagle. Whole-wheat bread is preferable to white bread, although it can be mildly laxative. Whole wheat contains all the germ and hulls of whole grain and is therefore richer in vitamin B, which more than makes up for its slightly lower digestibility. Always feed dogs stale (but not moldy) bread.

Dog biscuits come in two forms—with or without meat. Most brands are made with poor-quality meat (mostly cracklings), which isn't tolerated too well by dogs and can in some instances cause a bad case of diarrhea. Never depend totally on dog biscuits to feed your beagle.

Cooked cereals generally constitute the main food given puppies and very young dogs. It's fine to use commercially prepared cereals that are unsweetened. Some are made of grain mixes, including wheat, buckwheat, and barley.

Rice, especially whole-grain rice, is a good source of carbohydrates, provided it is well cooked.

Soy pellets are a good protein source and a good source of roughage. The pellets are specially treated with superheated steam under pressure to make them more digestible.

Other vegetables should always be boiled as little as possible, in as little water as possible. I provide them straight from the pan between other elements of the meal. You can use almost any kind of vegetable. Vegetables generally contain a good amount of vitamins and minerals.

Fats and Oils

Fats and oils are essential to the dog's diet even though too much fat can be harmful. Fat is a carrier for certain vitamins and essential fatty acids. Young dogs need fat as much as older ones; just consider the relatively high fat content of canine milk. There are a number of fat sources.

Dog biscuits (with meat) are generally high in fat.

Vegetable oils (from sunflowers, soybeans, and corn) are a good source of essential fatty acids.

Rendered animal fat (lard, tallow, etc.) is high in saturated fats and cholesterol. It contains few essential fatty acids.

Vitamins and Minerals

Vitamins and minerals, which are absolutely essential for the health of your beagle, are generally supplied in adequate quantities by a well-balanced diet. If supplementation seems indicated, baker's yeast or brewer's yeast is a good addition to consider. It contains many vitamins, including the B complex and vitamins D and E.

Commercial Dog Food

Commercial dog food can save you a lot of time and trouble. You don't have to worry about balancing your beagle's rations. You also don't have to be concerned about contamination with germs of all kinds. Homemade feed is easily contaminated, and is often unbalanced. Commercial preparations are made with strict quality control and can be trusted to remain germ free.

The shelf-life of commercial dog feed allows you to buy a good supply of food without worry about spoilage. You can put it in the pantry without need for precautions. The manufacturer takes this responsibility out of your hands.

By contrast, if you prepare your dog rations, you must constantly be on guard against spoilage. Meat and vegetables especially are highly perishable. You can preserve them by special processing, like cooking or freezing, but in practice this involves quite a bit of trouble. A notable and dangerous contaminant is *Salmonella* bacteria.

The shelf-life of commercial food is always indicated on the labels of standard brands. Be sure that you take note of the pull date, so that you gain the full benefit of freshness. Buy only the amount of food in advance that can be used up before the expiration date.

Dried dog food can be provided on a free-access basis, meaning that the beagle itself is allowed to determine the amount of food it consumes. A supply is made available day and night. In the beginning, a dog given free access to food is apt to overeat, but after a few days this will taper off. The dog acquires a sense of how much food it really needs. Free access to food is, naturally, easier on the owner; also, it can improve the pet's metabolism and temperament.

A young dog can learn to use a self-feeder at about four weeks of age. If you switch an

Puppies must be fed several times a day. Ask your veterinarian for advice if you are not sure about certain brands.

older dog to self-feeding, do it all at once. Make sure that a self-feeding dog always has a supply of fresh, clean drinking water and enough exercise.

Acceptability is one of the potential problems with commercial dog food. Not all types are accepted by a particular dog. It is a question of individual differences in liking certain tastes and smells. Fortunately, there is more than enough variation in the types of dog food that are available.

Types of Dog Food

In view of the wide variety of products on the commercial market, it is worthwhile to give this subject closer attention.

Dried feed can generally be provided without further preparation. It comes in dehydrated pieces, pellets, and balls that contain no more than 10 to 12 percent moisture. If you use it, your beagle will drink more than if you feed moist food, but that doesn't mean that it

should drink excessively. If excessive water intake does occur, switch to another kind of feed. If your beagle still drinks too much, consult your veterinarian.

Most commercial dried feed provides complete nutrition and furnishes all the required food elements.

Let's look in more detail at the various forms in which you can buy dried dog food.

Dog biscuits are baked into the familiar bone-shaped or square pieces. The type that contains meat generally has cracklings in it, which are poorly tolerated by many dogs and can cause severe diarrhea. The meatless biscuit can be combined with fresh or canned meat, separately or mixed together. Check the label to see whether the biscuit you're buying is intended as a complete food or should be supplemented. Dog biscuits and bits make a good snack for your beagle and can be given as a reward for good behavior.

Extruded or compressed dried feed is manufactured by grinding and mixing the constituents and then putting them, in the form of a mash, through a sieve under pressure. The diameter of the holes in the sieve determines the eventual size of the pieces, which are made in different sizes for young and adult dogs.

Expanded dried feed is manufactured by grinding and mixing the constituents and then forcing the mash under pressure through a tube with a gradually tapering diameter. When the mash reaches the small end of the tube, the pressure is suddenly released, causing the product to swell.

This process has the advantage of promoting digestibility. It also mixes the ingredients better, and because the product is hard, it promotes mechanical cleaning of your beagle's teeth.

Dog dinners are another variant of the complete, dried feed. Some of the ingredients remain in their normal, unground form, including expanded corn, rolled wheat, and pieces of dried vegetables. The other ingredients are added in the form of little pieces.

These dinners fill the demand of dog owners who want to give their pets a warm meal of the type they themselves enjoy. The dinner is prepared by pouring warm water or warm milk over it and letting it soak.

The moist dinner doesn't provide natural cleaning for your beagle's teeth; in fact, the food tends to stick between the teeth. You can counteract this by giving your beagle a rawhide or nylon bone and brushing its teeth regularly (see page 29).

Soft-moist and semimoist feed are complete rations with high digestibility. The biologic rating of soft-moist feed is generally somewhat higher than that of meat, and it is excellent for your beagle. The moisture content of soft-moist feed lies between that of dried feed and canned feed, about 25 percent. Almost all dogs like it, probably because it more closely resembles meat. It is a general rule that dogs like a food to the extent it resembles meat—and the moister, the better!

Canned food retains about 75 percent of the natural moisture in meat and vegetables. The well-known brands contain meat that was subjected to scientific quality control and broken into small pieces. Weighed quantities of meat

are mixed with about 20 other constituents. This variety promotes a high nutritional value.

Supplement canned food with hard biscuits, which help scour the dog's teeth.

Feeding Puppies

Before birth, the developing puppy is fed via the umbilical cord. The mother beagle provides it with all the nourishment needed for its growth. This all changes at whelping. The umbilical cord is severed, and the puppy has to feed itself. Once mother beagle has licked it dry, it gropes its way to the new source of nourishment. When it has reached the environs of the teats, the puppy makes upward motions with its head until it has found a nipple.

A healthy puppy naturally takes the nipple in its mouth and enjoys long drafts of warm milk. Its front legs make small kicks against the

All dogs enjoy an occasional treat.

TIP

Vitamin Cautions

Don't supplement complete feeds with extra vitamins and minerals. The manufacturer has carefully put in the right amounts of these items, and providing more can be dangerous for your beagle.

teats, which, along with the sucking, releases a hormone that stimulates milk production. The puppy's actions also stimulate contraction of the uterus, which promotes the speedy delivery of any puppies that still are in the womb.

During the first two days of lactation, the mother dog produces colostrum which is high in protein and rich in antibodies. The antibodies protect the little ones from infectious diseases against which the mother has been vaccinated, or from which she has recovered. It is quite important for puppies to receive this colostrum.

How long maternal antibodies protect puppies can be determined by serological analysis. It depends principally on the quantity of antibodies available in the female's blood. Generally, you can assume that puppies are protected until about the seventh week of age. In any event, I suggest you check with your veterinarian as soon as possible to arrange for vaccination, if this wasn't administered by the breeder.

Make sure that the mother dog lactates properly. If not, you will have to step in and help (see page 57). You can tell whether each puppy is developing properly by weighing the litter every day. If one of the puppies falls behind in weight, supplement the mother's milk with bottle feeding.

For beagle puppies, an ordinary baby bottle is fine. Be sure that the opening in the nipple isn't too large or too small and that the milk flows through it readily.

Artificial milk formula can be bought commercially, in powder form or completely ready to feed. The powder can be kept fresh longer, but you have to mix it with water. Be sure to follow the manufacturer's directions carefully.

You need a good thermometer to be sure that you provide the milk at the right temperature: 98.4° to 102.2°F (37°–39°C).

If your puppy won't take an artificial nipple, start it off with a few drops of milk placed on the tongue.

If a puppy stops drinking from the bottle it may well be that it has had enough, or it may just be fooling around. You can tell the difference by pulling the nipple partway out of its mouth. If it is still hungry, it will start sucking again. Also, be guided by the directions furnished by the manufacturer on how much and how often puppies should be fed.

Supplementary Feeding

About three to four weeks after birth, you must supplement the feed of all puppies. A great many beagle breeders start with a combination of cooked cereal and ground meat. You can make up the hot cereal from a combination of old brown bread, oats, and the like, in milk. The most commonly used meat is cooked ground beef.

If you want to get the puppies used to eating by themselves as soon as possible, it's best to keep the hot-cereal phase as short as possible. Switch to a commercial feed, soaked in milk if desired. Most commercial puppy feed is of high quality.

When you start supplementing the feed of your puppies, also be sure to provide water. Use a shallow puppy-sized bowl so that there's no chance of the puppy's drowning in it.

Depending on the size of the litter, furnish food three to six times per day.

Some females are in the habit of regurgitating food for their puppies at this stage of their development. This looks awful but is quite normal for dogs. They act just like wild canids that regurgitate partially digested feed for their young. Puppies seem to like eating it, and they often stimulate their mother to regurgitate by licking her around the snout.

Once puppies are around six weeks old, the mother beagle will have stopped lactating almost completely and will pay less attention to her litter. Typically, the mother will have kept the whelping box quite clean, but this cleanliness diminishes at the time of supplementary feeding. This means more work for the breeder.

Feeding Growing Dogs

Typically, young beagles get a new home some time after weaning. If you are the new owner, be sure to ask the breeder how he or she has been feeding the puppies. It is important that the dog receive the same food in the beginning as it did in its "old home." If you want to switch to another type of feed, do it very gradually (over a period of 4 to 5 days) and with appropriate care.

Stick to a complete feed, don't overfeed, and follow your veterinarian's advice regarding vitamin and mineral supplementation. Carefully observe your pet's eating habits.

Gradually, the young beagle can get the same feed as the grown dog, although in different quantities. I recommend weighing the animal from time to time and checking the weight against the recommended weight for its age according to the standard table you can get from your veterinarian.

When putting out feed and water for your beagle, be sure that you place the bowls at chest height. This keeps the dog from crouching while eating or drinking.

Feeding the Grown Dog

You can use a complete dog food year after year without problems, if it is a good-quality brand. Be guided by the beagle's preferences, which you will have discovered by now. Our modern world moves fast, so you may find that your favorite dog food is replaced by another product. I wouldn't worry much about this, because it is likely to be an improved product, given the competition in the market.

Feeding Pregnant Dams

During the first three weeks, the puppies don't grow much, but during the second half of the pregnancy, they grow rapidly and take in about twice as much foodstuff as during the first half. Consult your veterinarian about the precise food requirements of the pregnant female beagle.

Remember that quality is even more important than quantity in considering the feeding of a pregnant bitch (female). Don't skimp on quality!

After whelping, the puppies must be nourished by dog milk, which again draws on the body of the mother (dam). Be sure to keep up quality nutrition for the lactating dam. Immediately after whelping, again consult your veterinarian.

RAISING BEAGLES

The decision to breed beagles should not be made lightly. It requires careful consideration of a number of important factors.

There are obviously many good reasons why one should *not* breed beagles, or any other breed for that matter. Each year, many tens of thousands of beagles are born. So there is a real danger that breed quality may suffer. One has to ask oneself: "Will there be a good home for all these merry little fellows?" Prior to breeding a litter of beagles the novice owner should consider whether or not he/she is fully prepared to take on all the responsibilities and high costs involved in raising a beagle.

Let's now turn to the mechanics of beagle breeding, whelping, and rearing.

The first and most important rule is not to let a female beagle breed before she has been in heat at least twice.

Estrus, and What to Do About It

Most beagle females first come into heat (estrus) when they are about nine months of age. Generally, they come back into heat every six months. You notice the onset of heat by the swelling of the vulva, the only externally visible female reproductive organ. Many females start to emit odors during this proestrus period. Attracted by the odor, males approach the female, sniff under her tail, and at times a male makes an attempt to mount. Generally, the female doesn't appreciate this attempt and growls at the male. At the start of true heat, the vulva swells to the maximum extent. This exudate is quite different from the menstrual bleeding of women. Human menstruation occurs during the degenerative phase of the changes in the wall of the womb, but the exudate of bitches flows during the proestrus phase. The bloody exudate continues about ten days. Internally, two important changes are occurring. First, several ova ripen in the ovaries, and second, the wall of the womb thickens so that it is ready to receive the resulting embryos if the ova are fertilized.

After ten days, the exudate becomes lighter in color, and several days later it can be completely clear. In this period, the estrus, breeding can take place.

Beagles can be stubborn, but that quality demonstrates character.

After 14 to 15 days the exudate practically stops. After that, the swelling of the vulva decreases, and three weeks after the onset of true heat everything appears to have returned to normal.

If your female beagle follows this typical pattern, she can be bred on the tenth through twelfth days.

Unfortunately, many females don't stick to this schedule. Some of them allow mounting on the third day of heat. Others won't permit mounting until the ninth to twelfth day. In most cases, the tenth day is best for a successful mating, but there is an enormous range of favorable days for breeding. You must determine the right days for your own female dogs.

The Stud

Males that have had several satisfactory matings can be considered acceptable studs and should be able to maintain the characteristics of the breed properly. If they hadn't done well in earlier matings, people would have stopped using them for breeding purposes.

The penis of the male dog has a somewhat unusual build. A small bone inside it keeps the penis fairly stiff even in periods without sexual stimulation. Also, the penis contains two areas that can expand considerably, especially the posterior of the two. During mating, this highly swollen segment is usually completely inserted into the vagina. The female can contract the muscles of the vagina quite strongly, preventing the male from retracting the penis (the so-called "tie"). The two are thoroughly locked, a situation that can persist for some time, ranging from several to 45 minutes. When the female calms down and relaxes, her vaginal

muscles also relax, and the engorged penis becomes more flaccid as the blood drains away. Then the penis can be withdrawn.

Mating

When a female is ready for mating, she stands still before a male and raises her tail and bends it sideways. This totally bares her vulva. The male rears up on his hind legs and clasps his forelegs around the belly of the female. Next, the male tries to direct his penis toward the vulva, an effort that the dog owner can assist.

To be sure that the female is properly impregnated, many breeders let her mate again two days later—naturally with the same male. The thought behind this practice is to ensure that viable sperm are present at the same time the ripe ova enter the oviduct.

Since egg cells mature gradually, however, you don't want to take a chance and let a female roam while she is in heat, even if she has already been mated. Some females are quite ready to let themselves be mounted again by a strange male. You find out about this when she gives birth: There may be different types of puppies in the litter! Obviously, the only way that you can be certain that this will not happen is by restricting your female until estrus has terminated.

Pregnancy

After mating, you have a nine-week wait. At first, there is no visible indication to assure yourself that a bitch is indeed pregnant. Gradually, however, the bitch gains weight and slows her activities. You may be able to notice movement of pups in the womb as early as the fifth week.

As previously stated, an average pregnancy lasts 63 days, but some deviation is possible. So that you have a better idea of when whelping will start, I suggest taking your dog's temperature three times per day, starting on day 55. You can use an ordinary rectal thermometer, and you should always have a helper assist you. Normal canine temperature is about 101.5°F (38.5°C). About 24 hours before whelping begins, you will see a sharp drop to below 98.6°F (37°C).

False Pregnancy

Females can fool you with a false pregnancy. For nine weeks, they can faithfully show all symptoms of pregnancy. At the end of this period, they even begin to prepare a nest and milk can flow from their nipples. But no pups appear.

This phenomenon is caused by a hormonal derangement that happens to persist about as long as a pregnancy. However, if you know your female hasn't been mated, you can suspect false pregnancy. Some bitches show signs of false pregnancy after every heat period. On the other hand, if you have arranged a mating, false pregnancy can lead to real disappointment. To clear any doubt, have your veterinarian examine your dog.

Preparations

Most pregnancies run their course without difficulty. Sometimes the hormonal shifts cause a female to have an increased appetite the first few weeks, but don't give in to it. The first couple of weeks, the embryos hardly grow at

all, and if you overfeed the mother, she gets fatter and more lethargic, which can cause problems at whelping.

During the second half of pregnancy and certainly the last three weeks, the female's appetite increases appropriately because at that time the fetuses grow enormously fast. In some cases, a bitch has to be fed two or even three times the normal ration.

About the sixth or seventh week of pregnancy, start getting the female accustomed to the whelping box and whelping room.

Signs that the pregnancy is coming to an end include nesting behavior. Often the female keeps rearranging the bedding in the whelping box. For example, she may scratch and tear the newspapers you put down. You will also be able to see her nipples swell. As stated, you should take her temperature two to three times per day after the 55th day. Also be sure to alert your veterinarian at least two weeks before you expect the puppies.

The equipment you'll want to get ready before whelping starts includes a sterilized, somewhat blunt pair of scissors, a navel bandage, a disinfectant, cotton balls, towels, and a scale. Many breeders don't bother with a scale, but I think it's important to monitor the body weight of puppies. At birth, beagles weigh between 8.8 and 12.3 ounces (250–350 g), and eight to ten days later, this weight should have

Selecting a Whelping Site

In deciding on a whelping spot, pick a quiet place. I would avoid such locations as a corner of the kitchen or den. I would also advise against using the garage or shed. Those places are too cold and drafty and too far away for you to be able to keep an eye on the litter. You might miss an early sign that something is going wrong.

Generally, I would choose a bedroom. From the viewpoint of the litter, the best bedroom is your own. With the whelping box placed there, you'll be able to keep a close watch over the litter without leaving your bed, but be prepared to cope with a lot of new, strange sounds. If you don't want your rest disturbed, you might want to select another bedroom. Many breeders do so.

doubled. You should weigh your pups daily and note their progress.

The Whelping Box

Dogs naturally nest in hollows, and they love a quiet, comfortable nesting place. It should be snug but not inaccessible for you. I suggest a whelping box about as long as it is wide and big enough to allow your beagle female to be stretched out along the sides. Measure her from the tip of the nose to the base of the tail.

Many breeders make a special effort to keep a bitch from lying on her pups because her relatively heavy weight could kill a little one. These people build a rail along the side of the box under which the pups can lie without danger. I don't consider this precaution essential for a mother dog with healthy reflexes, but the rail certainly can't do any harm.

The sides of the box should be high enough so the beagle can stand up straight. Maintain at least this height if you want to put a cover on the whelping box. A lid isn't essential, however, and you definitely should not use one if you want to warm the box with a heat lamp. High walls are good. They prevent drafts, which are even worse for puppies than cold temperatures per se.

Cut the top down on one of the sides so the female can get in and out of the box easily, or provide a removable side. When the pups are just whelped, you can put a single slat across the opening to keep them in. Add a second slat when the pups become older and more exploratory. Still later, add a third slat.

A good heat source is important. Some people use an infrared lamp or a pig lamp, but

Puppies may look alike but typically have different personalities.

These active and playful puppies are "just doing their thing."

I don't recommend this type of heater. It radiates heat from only one direction, so that pups that don't move around much may get too hot on one side and too cold on the other side of their bodies. This can cause real problems in itself. Also, these ray lamps create dry air, which really is bad for the pups.

Contact heat is better, and you can provide it with a large heating pad. These electrically heated pads are at least 39½ × 23½ inches (100 × 60 cm). Some brands have a thermostat to adjust the heat; others are not adjustable. Install the pad under the whelping box so that about half the floor space is heated. In winter, I recommend placing the whelping box within a few feet of the radiator.

Keep the temperature of the floor of the box at about 75.2°F (24°C) for the first 10 to 14 days after whelping. After that, you can reduce the temperature gradually until it reaches room temperature at the end of the third week.

The best bedding for the whelping box is newspaper. The ink can rub off on the dog, but that doesn't really matter. Newspaper is quite absorbent. During the birth process, a lot of amniotic fluid is released, so that highly absorbent bedding is particularly important.

You can improve the bedding after whelping by placing a sheet or blanket over the paper. Be sure to change the cover frequently, as well as the bedding. Wash the cover in hot water.

Birth

Just before whelping, most beagle mothers are quite nervous, especially if they haven't had young before. They pace nervously, scratch at the bedding until the newspapers are shredded, and jump up and then drop down heavily. They pant hard. No one can help notice that something is going to happen.

Birth itself begins with contractions. The pressure moves the pups in the direction of the vagina, which now functions as a birth canal.

The birth of the first puppy is usually announced by rupture of the amniotic sac, which liberates a quantity of liquid. No matter how hard the female has to work to deliver her pups, she still finds time to frequently lick her vulva and lap up the amniotic fluid.

Generally, pups are born with the forelegs first followed by the head, but don't get upset if the hind legs come out first. Generally, a reverse birth causes no problems in dogs. With one or two strong contractions, the puppy is pushed entirely free.

Many bitches lie down during whelping, and the newborn puppy is shoved along the floor. Others give birth standing up, so that the puppies fall a certain distance to the floor. The fall seems scary to the onlooker, but almost every puppy survives it. So, don't worry.

Aftercare

Puppies can come into the world undraped, but often they are wrapped in part of the amniotic sac. Be sure to take off those pieces of membrane, especially from the puppy's head. You want to be sure nothing interferes with proper breathing. The mother dog usually takes care of this, but sometimes a bitch is so nervous that she tends to neglect her newborn. When she gives signs that she doesn't have a good sense of what is going on, you have to jump in to help.

Next, the umbilical cord has to be severed. Most puppies are born together with the placenta, or afterbirth, which is eaten by the mother dog. Before she does this you should tie off the cord and cut it. Don't let the mother bite it off. Use the blunt scissors you prepared for the purpose, and cut the cord about $7/8$ to $1\frac{1}{4}$ inches (2–3 cm) from the pup's belly. Blunt scissors squeeze the blood vessels as you cut.

As soon as a puppy gets up, it must be dried off. Most beagle dams lick off their young diligently and often rather roughly. This makes the puppies cry. Actually, the cries provide assurance that the puppy is alive and well.

If the dam neglects her puppies, dry them yourself with a towel. Feel free to rub. Just stroking the puppy with the towel doesn't dry it properly.

Also pay attention to the mouth, especially if a puppy has had a difficult birth. If the process took a long time, it may have swallowed some amniotic fluid. That's not bad if it is swallowed. If some leaked into the lungs, however, the puppy may be uncomfortable. You will know this is a potential problem if you see a lot of liquid and slime in the little mouth. This must be removed, and forcefully so. Rub the puppy dry; then take solid hold of it so that it can't squirm, and swing it several times, head down. The motion of the swing and the force of gravity will remove most of the slime and liquid from the mouth.

As soon as the puppy is dry and breathes quietly, lay it alongside the mother beagle. Some newborn pups seem extremely hungry and immediately look for a nipple. The sucking stimulates the mother beagle hormonally to give birth to the following puppies. So you can let the puppy suck without worry, but do stay in the neighborhood.

At the following birth, a mother may start pacing and turning, and the first-born pup may get in the way. Although a newborn puppy seems to be able to take a lot of abuse, it can be killed if it has to bear the brunt of its mother's full weight. That's why many breeders remove pups as they are born and lay them together in a nice, warm cozy corner until the entire litter has been delivered.

Successive puppies are born just like the first one. First you see the amniotic fluid, then the puppy. The new pup has to be dried and swung around if slime has to be removed from its little mouth. Meanwhile, the mother beagle eats the afterbirth which contains hormones that can favorably affect the birth process. However, the afterbirth may also cause digestive upsets. Instead, ask your veterinarian about an injection to provide the needed hormonal simulation.

Sometimes, a dam wants to take a break after the birth of a puppy and the processing that goes with it. It's all right to let the beagle out to exercise, urinate, and defecate. Encourage her to relieve herself, because a full bladder or intestine interferes with proper whelping. You want to provide all the internal room possible to let the puppies pass easily. During such a break, you can also give the dam some water to drink.

Successive births follow one another at changing intervals. A couple of puppies can be born very closely together, but generally the interval lasts a half-hour or longer. If the interval extends to more than two or three hours, the veterinarian can give the mother an injection to stimulate the contractions. Or, he or she may conclude the mother needs a cesarean. Another outcome may be that the veterinarian concludes tentatively that all the pups have

been whelped. I call this a "tentative" conclusion because the veterinarian can't feel puppies that may be left far back inside the pelvis and may also have a problem feeling those that lie far toward the front, inside the rib cage.

The entire whelping process may seem to take an eternity, but after several hours of real time, things quiet down. Let the mother beagle out for some exercise, and meanwhile take the little ones out of the box and clean it for them. When the mother beagle returns, put the puppies at her nipples and let them suck and rest.

The Checkup

When you have caught your breath, think of items of care you may have overlooked. Did you weigh the puppies at birth? If not, do it now.

Check each puppy carefully. They are born with closed eyes, which after 10 to 11 days open slowly.

The nose should be sound. A small split in the nose may point to a split palate, which may occur even if there isn't a true harelip. Look inside the mouth to make sure. Don't keep puppies with a harelip. They have real trouble sucking and starve if you don't have them euthanized.

Next, check the abdomen. With a little practice, you'll be able to sex the puppies. Young males don't show testicles, but the penis lies considerably more forward than does the vulva of the females. Be sure not to confuse the navel stem for a penis.

Finally, check the tail and anus. The first day of life, you will see the *meconium* coming out of the anus. This refers to the waste products that accumulated in the intestines during the

Healthy beagle puppies grow rapidly, are easygoing, and clean.

A properly proportioned beagle is typically healthy and robust.

fetal period. It must be eliminated before the puppy gets a good appetite to start sucking.

If you notice anything wrong, consult your veterinarian immediately!

Cesarean Operations

If your veterinarian had to help assure safe whelping by doing a cesarean, you'll have extra work with aftercare. The dam will still be dazed from the anesthesia, while the puppies are active and hungry. You will have to help feed and care for them for one or two days. Lay them at the nipples, and after they have sucked, massage their bellies and around the anus. Use moist cotton balls for this job. They need the massage to induce them to urinate and defecate. If you don't massage them, they become constipated, which can be a fatal problem in young pups.

Nursing

Colostrum

Colostrum is the first milk produced by the dam. It contains antibodies against all the diseases for which the mother was inoculated or from which she has recovered. During their first 36 hours of life, the puppies take in these antibodies, which then protect them against these diseases.

If the mother doesn't lactate during the first 36 hours, the puppies miss important protection. You will have to make up for this as much as possible. Maintain excellent hygiene, and don't allow your puppies near strange dogs. Consult with your veterinarian so you can have the puppies vaccinated at the earliest effective time.

Beagle puppies know where to go for nourishment.

Poor Lactation

You have to hand-raise the puppies if the mother lactates poorly or not at all, or in the sad case that she dies during whelping.

For a complete milk substitute, use commercially prepared milk powder. Some brands are about as good as real dog's milk. You need only add boiled and cooled water. Feed the puppies by letting them suck from bottles, which are available commercially.

Puppies need to drink frequently, especially at first. Expect to feed them every two to three hours. After seven to ten days, you can cut down the frequency provided the puppies are growing and gaining properly. Strong puppies can be fed every five to six hours. You'll know they're doing all right if they don't whimper hungrily but snooze and snore quietly in the box.

Remember to keep massaging the bellies with moist cotton balls after every meal. Make broad strokes across the belly from the ribs to the pelvis, mimicking the action of the dam's tongue. If they start to urinate and defecate, you'll know you have done it right. Don't worry, however, if there is no defecation after each meal. Sometimes the puppies urinate only.

Caring for the Puppies

Sometimes a litter seems to pine away within a week after whelping. The puppies don't gain, but lose weight. After a week to ten days they are so weak that they start dying. If this happens, consult your veterinarian immediately.

A possible problem may be incompatible blood types. If the dam is A negative and some or all of the puppies are A positive, she builds up antibodies to the puppies' blood. After whelping, these antibodies appear in the colostrum. Puppies drinking the antibodies do poorly because the antibodies break down the pups' red blood corpuscles. Perhaps CHV (herpes) might be the culprit. If caught early, some pups may be saved. Consult your veterinarian!

Other causes are harder to pin down. If the puppies have a virus infection, then something can be done for them. Other than providing environmental support, however, you can't do much for many weak pups.

Environmental support consists of temperature control. First, raise the ambient temperature in the whelping box to about 87°F (30°C). After three weeks, lower it gradually to 68°F (20°C).

More common is the situation in which a mother decides to do away with a runt. You'll see the little one lie at the dam's backside instead of at the nipples. Apparently, the runt is neglected because of its low body temperature. The usual temperature of puppies is normally one to two degrees lower than that of the mother beagle. If a puppy is cold or is poorly nourished, its temperature can drop to below 87°F (30°C).

If you want to improve a puppy's chances of living, you need to warm its body slowly. It won't do to put it under a heat lamp. That causes the puppy to dry out. It's better to warm it by holding it against your own body.

Next, see to it that the puppy has energy for producing its own body heat. It won't work to

have the mother beagle nurse it. I also advise against giving milk substitute to the puppy. The puppy won't be able to digest it because its stomach temperature is even lower than its basic body temperature. If you get milk into the stomach, the milk curdles.

You need to make up a special sugar solution. Put glucose and a pinch of salt into water that was boiled and then cooled. Keep the temperature of the solution at least at body temperature—about 98.6°F (37°C). Drip some of the solution into the puppy's mouth, at first every 15 minutes, then every 30 minutes, and finally every hour. By the way, the reason for putting a little salt into the solution is to help prevent dehydration. The very effective method of tube feeding can also be used.

The whole process of warming the puppy and feeding it by hand can take many hours. You need to stay with the little one until it shows activity and can raise its head. Then you can put it back into the box with its mother. If she then accepts it, you have saved its little life!

When the Eyes Open

During their first ten days of life, puppies are completely helpless. They feel their way through the whelping box and generally know to find their source of milk. If they stray too far from the mother beagle, she can take the puppies in her mouth and bring them back where they ought to be.

About the tenth or eleventh day, the eyes slowly open. The process can take a few days; one eye can be ahead of the other.

The opening of its eyes ushers in a new stage of life for a puppy. It has to absorb many more impressions than it did the first ten days. The puppy becomes more curious and starts crawling farther away from the mother beagle. However, don't change the daily care and feeding until about the twentieth day.

Worming and Supplementary Feeding

Many puppies are born with an infestation of intestinal roundworms. Puppies should be wormed with a mild product, such as Nemex II, for the first time at the age of two or three weeks; after that, repeat wormings every two weeks or so until the puppies are fully weaned and their stool samples are clear. If you are acquiring an older puppy, ask the breeder if it has already been wormed.

You should get ready to start supplementary feeding at about three weeks. Part of the supplement can be baby cereal, which you should prepare with dog milk substitute.

About the same time, you can get the puppies accustomed to solid food. Many breeders offer a small portion of cooked hamburger meat, starting the third week. You can also use finely sliced canned meat or soft-moist feed. Dry feed can't be handled by puppies at that age, not even if it is soaked in milk or water.

Weaning

Expect lactation of the female to decrease between the third and sixth weeks after whelping. Increase supplementary feeding accordingly. About the sixth week, puppies should be ready for weaning, so during the previous three weeks you will have to gradually increase the amount of meat, soft moist feed, or canned food, along with a serving of cereal from time to time. Provide water for drinking.

The amount of food needed by puppies of that age is considerable, but the size of their stomachs is relatively small. I strongly suggest you provide four to six meals per day, even though it is more work than feeding once or twice daily.

Around the sixth week, you can separate the puppies from their mother. Many breeders give the puppies a great degree of freedom at this point and let the mother dog join her puppies only when she herself feels like it. When the puppies get the chance, they will rush toward their mother in order to try to suckle again. Most mothers won't have any milk to give or very little, but that doesn't keep the little ones from trying.

At this stage, the pups have developed teeth, and sucking can hurt their mother's nipples considerably, so mother beagle will not enjoy being with her pups for very long. You can remove her from their quarters to give her relief. You can build some kind of platform to which the mother can jump. Puppies of that age can run well but they can't jump much at all. From her perch, the mother beagle can watch them without being stormed!

Leave-taking

You can have the new owners pick up their puppies when they are eight to nine weeks old. Saying good-bye to the little ones can tug at your heartstrings. After all, you just spent eight to nine weeks raising the pups from newborns to young dogs, and with all the effort you put into the task, you surely will have become attached to them. Good sense tells you that you must let them go nonetheless.

IF YOUR BEAGLE GETS SICK

The ultimate responsibility for your beagle's health is yours, but clearly you can't take care of everything yourself. Your most important adviser is your veterinarian.

You have a broad choice of veterinarians, but once you select one, I suggest you stick with him or her as long as you don't have a well-founded reason for changing.

Be reasonable in dealing with your veterinarian. The fact that you pay for services doesn't give you the right to telephone at impossible hours for a consultation—certainly not if your dog has been sick for some time.

Your veterinarian should be able to expect certain things from you. You ought to have basic knowledge about the health care of your beagle, including worming, parasite control, vaccination, and nutrition.

By creating a healthy environment and by taking preventive steps, you can protect your beagle from many injuries and maladies.

Disorders of the Coat and Skin

Beagles shed normally every spring and fall to exchange winter fur for summer fur. Abnormal hair loss does, however, occur as well and can be caused by one of the following: poor feeding, eczema, parasites, a generally poor condition after illness, and hormonal disturbances.

Symptoms can include itch, bare spots, and repeated shedding. Ask your veterinarian for the right treatment. He or she will look into the following:

✔ The feeding of the beagle can cause a reaction on the skin and coat. Reactions to pork, horse meat, herbs, and seasonings are particularly common. Dogs should definitely not be given too much fat.

✔ Several types of eczema may be caused by excessive carbohydrates in the diet. In any event, leave treatment of eczema to your veterinarian, who will cut the remaining hair from the affected spots, clean the area, and recommend medication against infection. He or she also may recommend an improved diet.

✔ Another possible cause is parasites, including fleas and lice (see pages 34–35) or worms (see pages 63–65). A much more serious parasite is the scabies mite *(Sarcoptes)*, which buries itself in the skin to lay its eggs. The infested dog scratches itself continuously, resulting in raw bare spots at the elbow, knee, and margins of the ear. If left untreated, the bare spots spread over the whole body.

Parasites must be fought with strong remedies. Your veterinarian will recommend treatment. To avoid further transmission, separate the affected dog from other animals and maintain proper hygiene. The environment must also be thoroughly cleansed; otherwise, the animal will be reinfected.

✔ Abnormal hair loss often occurs after serious illness. It certainly will help to gradually restore the normal condition of the coat with a proper, accurately balanced diet.

✔ Baldness (alopecia) in puppies may be caused by a deficiency of thyroxine (thyroxine is an iodine-containing hormone produced by the thyroid gland to regulate metabolism), resulting from an iodine deficiency in the diet of the dam. In any event, consult a veterinarian for advice. Prevent the problem by feeding a pregnant beagle properly.

The mother dog may have problems with baldness after whelping, caused by hormonal changes. Again, proper feeding can remedy this quickly.

Of course, should the condition persist after several weeks of highly nutritious feeding,

it is advisable that you consult with your veterinarian.

Disorders of the Digestive System

Constipation

If your beagle doesn't defecate "on schedule," there's no reason to be alarmed immediately. You don't need to intervene until the trouble has continued for three days. Then add one of the following to the feed: Metamucin or Mucilose. These are over-the-counter products—available without prescription.

Diarrhea

Diarrhea is caused mainly by various infectious diseases, poor feeding, poisoning, "colds," and intestinal worms. The stools are thin, sometimes mucus-laden, and there may even be blood in serious cases.

Most cases of mild diarrhea can be cured by restricting your pet to weak tea, rice, or rice water for a day. If necessary, medicate the dog with charcoal tablets. Once the diarrhea diminishes, gradually resume normal feeding, provided that this food is proper and is not the cause of the diarrhea.

In a serious case of diarrhea, with mucus and blood, you should always consult your veterinarian. In all cases, be sure that the sick beagle lies in a warm place.

Anal Sacs

The anal sacs have small openings that become visible by slightly curling the anus outward. You can notice the two openings at 5 and at 7 o'clock, viewing the anal opening as a watch. The glands continually produce a nasty-smelling fluid that is stored in the sacs until emptied during defecation. The dog can also squeeze the fluid out of the sacs when danger threatens. In other words, the anal sacs function precisely like the scent glands of the skunk. When the anal sacs do not empty normally, they go from being full to being overfilled (impacted). The dog responds by licking under its tail. If that doesn't bring relief, the animal pulls its anus along the ground. We call this symptom "scooting," in which the animal sits, raises its hind legs and pulls itself along with its forelegs.

Scooting can also be caused by other problems, such as feces adhering to the anus, undigested grass that hangs partially out of the rectum and anus, and small wounds. To determine the true cause, examine the beagle under the tail. If the anal sacs are impacted, you can often see a small bump on either side of the anus.

Scooting along the ground scrapes the openings of the anal sacs, and the resulting damage allows bacteria to enter. These can bring about a nasty infection that will require treatment by your veterinarian.

A common side effect of an infection of the anal sacs is a bare back. The affected dog has a terrible itch and scrapes itself wherever it can. Generally the bare spot develops on the rump. This is the same spot that is chafed bare when a dog has fleas. So if you see a bare back, remember to look not only for fleas but also for problems in the anal sacs. If the anal sacs are overfilled, they must be emptied manually—a job best left to your veterinarian. Remember, if this isn't done, there may be all kinds of complications.

Anal sac infections can be cured by medication. Some veterinarians also advise an operation to remove the sacs altogether.

Worms

The most common intestinal worms are tapeworms and roundworms.

Tapeworms

Tapeworms attach themselves with the head (*scolex*) to the mucous membranes of the intestines and absorb nourishment. The head is connected to a chain of segments (*proglotids*). The segments, each of which contains a large number of eggs, are excreted with the feces.

Dogs can be infested by at least seven types of tapeworms, one of which, the *Echinococcus* tapeworm, is definitely dangerous to humans. All tapeworms live in the small intestine. Every species of tapeworm has a specific intermediate host for its life cycle. These can be fleas, lice, sheep, pigs, rabbits, dogs, or even fish.

The symptoms of tapeworm infestation are obvious only in serious cases. They include weight loss (despite a good diet), excitability, cramps, and sometimes diarrhea. You can detect the segments of tapeworm in the stools as small white pieces. You can also see

TIP

A Word Regarding Worming

Consult your veterinarian for details about proper worming procedures. If not done correctly, worming prior to whelping could cause abortion!

Beagles are normally strong and healthy, with lots of stamina.

them as dried pieces resembling rice kernels in the hairs around the anus. Immediately consult a veterinarian. He or she will prescribe remedies against the worm as well as against any fleas present.

Roundworms

Roundworms are sturdy and white, ranging in length from 2 to 4 inches (5–10 cm), with the females longer than the males. They also appear in the small intestine.

The eggs are excreted with the stools. When a dog takes in such an egg, it lodges in the intestine. There the egg develops into a larva, which drills itself through the intestinal wall into the bloodstream, by which it is carried to the lungs. It stays there for some time and then travels via the respiratory system to the throat. It is swallowed and then settles in the intestines, where the larva matures to the adult stage.

Damage to the lungs and liver during the process can cause infections. As symptoms, look for digestive disturbances of all types, changing appetite, constipation, diarrhea, intestinal infections, and sometimes also a vomiting of worms. Pups have a hard, swollen belly; they walk with legs apart, cough, grow thin, and develop a dull coat.

Immediately consult a veterinarian. Prevent infestation by keeping the dog quarters properly clean. Remove feces and disinfect the kennels daily. Examine beagles regularly for worms. Breeding bitches must be wormed ten days before whelping and ten days after whelping.

Hookworms and Whipworms

Hookworms and whipworms are common internal blood-sucking parasites. Hookworms have hooked mouth parts with which they fasten themselves to the intestinal walls of the dog, causing the disease ancylostomiasis. The larvae are activated by the hormonal changes of pregnancy and are carried into the embryos by the bloodstream.

Many infestations occur by way of worm eggs that already-infested animals pass in the stool.

The symptoms of infestation are bloody diarrhea, loss of appetite, vomiting and anemia, and pale gums.

Take the patient to your veterinarian at the first sign of illness (and take a stool sample along in a tightly closed container).

Heartworms

Heartworms are transmitted by mosquito bites and live in the right ventricle and pulmonary artery of the heart of dogs and other mammals. Heartworms, which are extremely dangerous internal parasites, can grow up to 12 inches (30.5 cm) in length.

The signs of heartworm disease include fatigue, labored breathing, frequent coughing, and faintness. Unfortunately, these symptoms are often not apparent until the disease has reached a grave stage. Since large parts of the United States and Canada are threatened by heartworm infestations, it is now common practice to maintain all dogs on a monthly heartworm prevention program. Consult your veterinarian.

Beagles are seldom noisy. Only when left alone do they tend to howl loudly.

Kennel Cough

Kennel cough is a misleading term, because this virus infection does not occur in kennels only. It is agreed that most infected dogs are indeed found in kennels, but all dogs, including house pets, can get it. Kennel cough is an infection of the throat, larynx, and trachea.

This highly contagious condition is caused by a virus, although it can be complicated by a bacterial infection as well. Affected dogs have a normal body temperature and remain normally active and alert.

The infection can be prevented by an attenuated vaccine, which normally is administered by the veterinarian in the standard puppy series and the annual booster shot. Dogs with kennel cough should be kept in a quiet place away from other dogs. All causes for barking should be avoided. There are no specific treatments, although cough suppressants are usually recommended.

I strongly suggest that you have the sick dog examined by a veterinarian to be sure it doesn't catch bronchitis. The veterinarian will certainly want to suppress this infection with antibiotics, because a lung infection can easily result.

Serious Diseases

Distemper

Canine distemper is a viral disease that strikes mainly young dogs but also can infect other animals, including raccoons, coyotes, skunks, and wolves. It poses no danger to humans.

The first symptoms of distemper are visible about five to eight days after the virus invades the body. At first, only the mucous membranes are affected. Common symptoms are coughing, sneezing, nasal discharge, teary eyes, and sometimes diarrhea and vomiting.

The virus then proceeds to invade other tissues and do damage there. At that point, a secondary bacterial infection can significantly worsen the disease picture. The lungs are particularly susceptible. Bronchitis, pneumonia, and pleuritis are possible. These complications can be so serious as to be fatal.

The most serious form of the disease appears after three to five days. The dog's temperature runs as high as 103° to 105°F (39.5°–40.5°C); immediate medical attention is required. Without it, distemper enters the nervous system. This brings about a variety of symptoms, rang-

ing from lameness to muscle spasms. In most cases, infections of the nervous system are fatal. Few dogs recover completely and most survivors are left with a disability.

No medicines are effective against distemper. Frequently, antibiotics are prescribed to fight the secondary bacterial infection, but these antibiotics have no effect whatever on the virus. The only medication for distemper is prevention, brought about by a well-planned vaccination schedule.

Authorities are virtually unanimous in advising that puppies be vaccinated against distemper by the time they are six weeks old. To maximize maternal protection during the first six weeks of life, vaccinate the female at the start of heat. By the time she is ready to be bred, protection is at its peak, and the mother dog can provide satisfactory levels of protection in her milk.

Your beagle will also require annual booster shots to keep the antibody level high.

Hepatitis

Hepatitis is a virus disease that is sometimes fatal. The infected animal loses its appetite, runs a fever, emits a bloody diarrhea, or vomits. It is quite obvious that the dog has abdominal pains.

Sometimes the disease has a rapid course: One day the dog looks completely healthy and the next day it is dead. It is clear that a veterinarian needs to be consulted immediately. He or she will administer antibiotics, intravenous fluids, and vitamins and may provide a blood transfusion or infuse other fluids.

Hepatitis can be prevented with an attenuated vaccine, which is commonly provided along with distemper vaccine. This is a remark-

TIP

Important Note
See your veterinarian immediately if your beagle is bitten by a wild animal or by a dog not immunized against rabies (see page 68).

It is also advisable to see the veterinarian if you cannot identify the dog that inflicted the bite.

Vaccination Schedule for Dogs*

Disease	Initial Vaccination	Boosters
Adenovirus 2**	6 weeks	8 weeks; annually
Bordetella**	6 weeks	8 weeks; every 6 months
Coronavirus	6 weeks	8 weeks; annually
Distemper	6 weeks	8 weeks; 16 weeks; annually
Hepatitis	6 weeks	8 weeks; 16 weeks; annually
Leptospirosis	6 weeks	8 weeks; 16 weeks; annually
Parainfluenza	6 weeks	8 weeks; 16 weeks; annually
Parvovirus	6 weeks	8 weeks; 16 weeks; 6 months or annually, depending on vaccine used.
Rabies	12–16 weeks	Second vaccination at about one year of age, depending upon local and state ordinances, with annual to triennial shots for the rest of the dog's life.

*The vaccination schedule will typically vary from one veterinarian to another, and within different locations of the country where risks may differ. Vaccinations are now available for Lyme disease, which may be recommended for the hunting/field trial beagle. Please consult your veterinarian.
**In part responsible for the "kennel cough" syndrome (see page 65).

ably effective vaccine. While it is thought that a single injection provides lifelong immunity, yearly boosters are recommended as standard procedure. After the booster shot, the dog is generally sluggish, loses its appetite, and runs an elevated temperature. There is no need to consult a veterinarian.

Leptospirosis

This kidney infection is caused by bacterial organisms (Leptospira species). It is infectious to humans and occurs in cattle and rats as well as dogs, raccoons, swine, and many other mammals.

The sick beagle has an obvious temperature, completely loses its appetite, has abdominal pains, vomits, loses weight, frequently shows a weakness of the hind legs, has diarrhea, and drinks a large volume of water.

The veterinarian administers antibiotics, the necessary fluids, and vitamins. To allow the kidneys the chance to heal properly, the veterinarian may perform peritoneal dialysis.

Proper vaccination with a yearly booster can also prevent this disease and its attendant problems. You may need more frequent boosters (up to six per year) if you live in areas with many infected rats or cattle. The disease spreads by contact with the urine of an infected animal or by drinking or swimming in contaminated water. After vaccination, beagles may exhibit the same symptoms as after a hepatitis booster.

Rabies

Rabies, or "hydrophobia," is caused by a fatal virus that is highly concentrated in the saliva of rabid animals, such as foxes, skunks, bats, raccoons, cats, and dogs. The virus was first identified by Louis Pasteur in 1881. Rabies is an acute infectious disease of the central nervous system. Many, if not all, warm-blooded animals can spread this disease, which is endemic in many countries. Rabies-free countries, such as Britain, Australia, and New Zealand, impose strict quarantine regulations to avoid its spread, and even a current vaccination certificate is

The beagle is generally a good-natured hound and is especially suitable as a family pet.

required when shipping your beagle across some state lines (ask your veterinarian).

No warm-blooded animal will get rabies until it is bitten by a rabid animal, or infected by a rabid animal's saliva through an open wound. In man, early symptoms include nausea, fever, malaise, and sore throat. Increased salivation and extreme sensitivity of the skin to temperature changes, of the eyes to light, and of the ears to sound are signs very important to early diagnosis.

The incubation period of the rabies virus is usually between 10 and 120 days, but sometimes up to six months, depending on the location of the bite and the time it takes the virus to reach the brain.

There are two types of rabies: *dumb rabies* (the dog is far from active, the mouth often hangs open, and there is apt to be a peculiar look in the eyes) and *furious rabies*. In the latter the dog is snappy and irritable, becomes restless, and wanders off to hide in dark places. It often howls and usually attacks and/or bites any human or animal that crosses his path. Seek veterinary attention immediately, and if anyone is bitten by a suspect dog (or other warm-blooded animal), clean the wound with soap or disinfectant at once and consult a physician without delay. Prompt action can save a life!

Rabies Reminder

There is no treatment for rabies once symptoms have developed in man or dog! Vaccinations against rabies are mandatory for all dogs (see Vaccination Schedule, page 67). This will protect your beloved animal and thus you and your family from this potentially fatal disease.

Pseudorabies

Pseudorabies, also known as Aujeszky's disease, is transmitted to dogs by infected pork. If pork is mixed with beef, this, too, can be infected.

Affected dogs become listless and may vomit and have diarrhea. Unfortunately it is irrevocably fatal for dogs. Dogs that consume infected pork often die as quickly as two or three days later. To date, there is no treatment.

Prevent infection by keeping dogs out of pig sties; the illness can be transmitted in infected urine. Never feed dogs raw pork. If you feed pork to dogs that are not allergic to it, boil it in water for at least half an hour. The virus poses no threat to humans.

Parvovirus

The parvovirus primarily attacks the bone marrow, immune system, and gastrointestinal tract, but it can also damage the heart. It is a serious killer, especially of puppies, but it can bring death to an unvaccinated or untreated dog of any age. Puppies with this disease can suffer from severe dehydration because of profuse bloody, watery diarrhea and vomiting, and may die within 48 hours of onset.

While good veterinary care can save some parvovirus victims, immunization followed by annual booster shots is a much better course of action.

Dog Diseases and Humans?

Yes! Diseases transmissible to humans include leptospirosis and rabies (if a rabid dog inflicts a bite). Therefore, it is always advisable to consult a veterinarian whenever it is unclear from what illness a dog is suffering.

Coronavirus

This contagious disease can cause severe diarrhea with watery, loose, foul-smelling, bloody stool. It may leave a dog in such a weakened condition that parvovirus or other infections may occur. Immunization by vaccine is the preferred course. By preventing this ailment, you may be able to avoid putting your pet at risk for more serious medical problems.

First Aid

Bites

Beagles are not the biting type, but they do sometimes bite humans or another animal. Males that are kept together in a kennel have been known to inflict painful bites on each other, frequently involving a torn ear. Bite wounds, including those on the ears, can bleed severely.

If your beagle suffers a small wound, wash it with a mild antiseptic. If it needs stitches, or if a wound seems to heal slowly, consult your veterinarian.

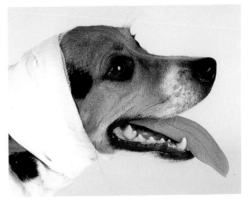

Sick or injured beagles should always be treated by a veterinarian.

Insect Stings

Beagles are extremely playful, and they love to chase bees and wasps. No wonder that beagles are subject now and then to a painful sting! Wash the stung area with a strong solution of bicarbonate of soda. Be sure to consult a veterinarian for stings on or near the nose, mouth, tongue, or eyes.

Frostbite

Frostbite, which makes the animal shiver and look sleepy, is rare in dogs, even in hunting hounds like beagles. If they have been outside in freezing weather for a long time, however, it is still quite possible that the margins of the ear, the tail, or the scrotum may be affected by frostbite. If you suspect this, put your beagle in a warm room. Place a hot water bottle (in a cover) in its dog bed or an electric pad or blanket if available. This helps raise the body temperature. Warm the affected parts with your hands or use a moist, warm towel (note that I said *warm*, not *hot!*). Under no circumstances should you rub or squeeze! Give the beagle warm liquids to drink, and check the rectal temperature every hour.

If the animal is unconscious, consult a veterinarian immediately.

Disorders of the Eyes

If your beagle suddenly closes its eyelids, it may have sand or other foreign bodies in the eye. Rinse the eye or eyes carefully with eyewash. If none is available, use tap water that has been boiled, cooled, and, if possible, filtered. Apply with a plastic syringe, which is available in the drugstore. Be sure not to touch the eyeball in the process. When you rinse, be sure you use more than enough rinsing liquid.

If your beagle continues to squeeze its eyelids (or there is no marked improvement), consult your veterinarian because you are probably dealing with an infection of the mucous tissue or a foreign body. Such an infection often results from drafts—for example, if your beagle was permitted to put its head out of the window of a moving vehicle.

Any eye irritation causes heavy tearing, but a heavy flow of tears can also be caused by a blockage in the tear ducts. A veterinarian can flush away the blockage. Stick to the following rule: If excessive tearing persists longer than two hours, consult your veterinarian immediately. A number of eye infections and disorders, such as glaucoma, should be treated only by a veterinarian. The so-called "cherry eye" concerns the prolapsed gland or the third eyelid, and is a common problem in beagles. Corrective surgery can tack the gland back into place.

To check the eye of a beagle, put your hands around your pet's head and apply gentle pressure to open the eyelid. Foreign particles can be flushed away carefully with eye wash.

Pulse and Heartbeat

As soon as the body temperature of a dog exceeds 103°F (39.5°C), it has a fever. This doesn't always mean that it is sick. The body temperature may rise somewhat because of excitement, or from riding in a hot car, among other reasons. You can take the temperature rectally.

To help establish whether your beagle may require a veterinarian's attention, you can also check the pulse on the left front paw, or on the upper inside of the thigh. Place your finger lightly on one of these spots for one minute and count the number of beats.

A healthy, grown dog has a pulse rate or heart rate of 70 to 90 beats a minute.

Euthanasia

If your beagle remains healthy and avoids serious accidents, the end of its days will probably occur between its twelfth and fifteenth year.

Unfortunately the saying "Old age has its infirmities" is all too true. An aged beagle tends to become slower in its movements. Its eyesight dims and its teeth fall out. It has trouble holding its urine and its feces, so that it needs to relieve itself more often. Serious illness can become a problem, and you may have to consult a veterinarian. Painkilling drugs can help, and often a carefully regulated diet will be beneficial. Generally, a beagle maintains its interest in food. Even in old age it will greedily attack its rations and swallow them with gusto to the last bite.

The aging process in beagles tends to be gradual, in contrast to the situation with large dogs, which can go from exuberance to infirmity within months. If no serious illness or infirmities occur, you can continue to enjoy your last years with your pet.

There are cases, however, in which an animal develops so many ailments that it requires almost constant attention without any clear sign that it will soon die naturally. In such cases, you must seriously consider the possibility of euthanasia. Discuss the situation thoroughly with your veterinarian. Let him or her give you a professional opinion about the remaining possibilities that your beagle's life can be extended for its pleasure and for yours. If no such possibilities remain, then euthanasia may be the best remaining course of action.

At that point, your dog has been your loyal friend and companion for many years, so it is only fair that you stay with it to its last breath and heartbeat. Your dog has the right to spend its last moments in your company.

You need not be afraid of the leave-taking. Death in the office of your veterinarian is a far from scary event. The veterinarian will use personal skills and medications to calm the beagle, so that it first falls into a deep sleep.

At that point, the breathing becomes shallower and the heart beats more slowly. The dog remains asleep until the end.

You will be left with an empty, sad feeling. After all, your faithful companion through the years has disappeared from your life forever. All you have are the memories.

SIMPLE OBEDIENCE TRAINING

Obedience training is a continuous process that takes place during the daily interaction between you and your beagle.

You and the other members of your family are the only ones who can effectively teach the beagle. Others can help; they can teach you how to teach your dog. But you have to do the real work yourself.

Basic Obedience for Pets

As a minimum, your pet should learn to walk alongside you properly while on a leash, to sit, to stay, to lie in a place you select, and to come when you call it. Other desirable "skills" for your beagle depend on your needs.

"Sit"

Many beagles sit down naturally when they want to look up at their master. You can use this tendency by saying *"Sit"* every time the

With proper training, a beagle can learn basic and advanced obedience skills.

beagle sits down on its own. After a while, the dog will make a connection between the word and its action.

This technique makes the beagle basically familiar with the command, but it isn't actually "obedience." A more direct approach is to kneel next to your puppy and hold its collar with your right hand. Then give it the command *sit*, and pull up its head somewhat with your right hand while, with the left, you gradually push down its rump, so that it is forced to sit down. As soon as the dog does this, stroke its head and back quietly and praise it. Say, "That's a good dog, that's '*sit*,'" or words to that effect.

If the dog gets the urge to rise, immediately put your left hand back on its rump, push it down, and correct the dog with "No. *Sit*." Then praise it again as soon as it sits completely.

When you push down the dog, keep your left hand as far back on the rump as possible. Many people make the mistake of putting their hand too far forward, so that, in effect, they push on the loins. This is less effective because you have to push harder, and it is also quite unpleasant for the dog. As a result, it may start to defy you, which naturally is not your intent.

At the start, don't let your dog sit for too long a time. After it sits properly for a little while, let it go with a pleasantly spoken command, "free," or whatever word you decide to use to signal release. Then play with your beagle a little while and let it romp around as a reward. Altogether, the *sit* lesson doesn't need to take more than two or three minutes. I strongly recommend keeping all lessons quite short for pups and other dogs starting obedience training. However, during that short time, work intensively. This way, the beagle learns the most, and you avoid the chance that the animal becomes bored. Feel free to repeat the *sit* lesson three or four times per day.

"Stay"

After several days, you won't have to put pressure on the dog's rump anymore; you will be able to stand up while you give the command. As you step away with your right foot, swing

your left palm down toward your pet's face almost far enough to touch the muzzle, and command *stay!* Slowly increase the length of time you have the beagle stay in place until you give it the command that releases it.

You don't need to set any records. At that stage of training, the most important thing is that your beagle respond immediately to your command and not move until you give the signal by saying "free"—or whatever.

It is important that your beagle perform the action on command perfectly at least once every day. If your dog obeys sometimes and other times gets up without permission and runs away, you may have asked more from your beagle than it could handle. Once this occurs you may find that your dog is almost *forced* to make mistakes constantly. Since you have to correct continually, your beagle rarely, if ever, receives praise. Very soon it loses all interest in working with you.

It helps to give the first *sit* and *stay* lessons in a quiet room, where there are few distractions. This way, the dog can take in more easily what you are trying to teach. Once the lesson goes smoothly indoors, you can start practicing with your beagle out of doors in a quiet environment. At the same time, you can commence indoors with the *heel* command.

"Heel"

Before you take your beagle out of doors on a leash, it should be used to wearing a collar

To teach the command stay, tell your beagle to sit, then step away with your right foot as you swing your left hand, palm down, toward the dog's muzzle and say, "Stay" in an emphatic tone of voice.

indoors. In general, this takes a day, or at most several days.

You can get your beagle puppy somewhat used to a leash indoors, also. Connect the leash to the collar and let the puppy drag it behind itself.

When you move out of doors, the puppy will rebel at first against the limiting freedom of the leash. It may make wild jumps, it may lie down or sit down, or it may try to walk backward and pull its head out of the collar. Walk along with your pup and keep the leash from being pulled taut. The puppy should know from the start that the leash is not intended for a "tug of war."

Soon the beagle will be accustomed to the leash. Then you can try to catch its attention with friendly talk. If the puppy starts walking along your left side, then praise it constantly: "That's a good dog. That's *'heel.'* Very good!" As long as it keeps walking on your left and the leash stays slack, keep praising the beagle constantly. If it tries to run off and the leash is pulled taut, get the dog to come back to you with one or more *brief* tugs while you give the command *heel* at short intervals. As soon as the beagle once again walks along with you properly, praise it lavishly.

Naturally you can't expect perfection from your puppy. The most important result of this lesson is that your puppy begins to understand clearly that it will constantly be rewarded if it walks along beside you.

Don't let this lesson go on too long, either. A few minutes at a time is really enough. Very

When "heeling," your beagle walks along on your left, its head about level with your left knee. When you practice turns, hold your beagle on a very short leash.

==== T I P ====

Additional Help

If you experience any difficulty teaching your dog to *heel* properly, you should go to an obedience-training course. The practical help that a good instructor can give can't be replaced even by a good book.

gradually, you can make the exercise somewhat more difficult. Then, for example, you can teach your beagle to sit down close to you as soon as you stand still. To make left and right turns, hold the dog on a very short leash. This forces your pet to turn with you. Command *heel* as you make the turn.

"Lie Down"

Lie down, or more simply *down,* can be a lifesaving command for your beagle. Sooner or later your dog will be off leash when a car is approaching. If you call the dog to come, you might call it in front of the wheels of the

left: These attentive dogs are eagerly awaiting their next command.

below: Get your beagle used to wearing a collar and being on a leash—both indoors and out.

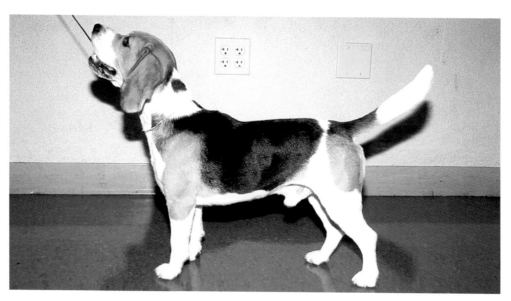

The beagle appears to understand and relish showing off.

oncoming car. It is far safer if you can get the beagle to stay where it is with the command *lie down,* appropriately followed by the command *stay.*

Lying down for someone of higher rank is a gesture of submission. If you force your beagle to lie down, this represents a gesture of domination, and your beagle may find the reason for it hard to understand. There's a good chance, therefore, that your dog will not react dependably while it is still learning the concept of *lie down.* Therefore don't impose this demand too forcefully, for it will inevitably make your dog more unsure.

Make good use of situations when your puppy lies down beside you on its own, perhaps to be stroked. Kneel down by the dog, and with a rather deep voice say *"Lie down"* while you quietly stroke it. Follow by saying "Good dog. That's *lie down. Stay.* Good dog." If the beagle then wants to get up, you can push it down again and repeat the command *lie down,* again followed by quiet conversation and strokes.

Don't let your puppy lift the command on its own. Keep it in position until you tell your dog "free," and then romp a little with it. Once again, however, don't let the training session last too long.

The next step is to kneel down by a dog that's standing, give the command *sit,* and take hold of a front leg with each of your hands and, by pulling gently, force the dog to lie while you give the command *lie down.*

As your puppy starts to understand better and better what the commands *lie down* and *stay* mean, gradually stop stroking the dog the whole time. Don't remain in a kneeling position, but get on your feet. You can still stand bent over your beagle, with a hand stretched down toward the dog. This is also a dominating gesture, but your dog should be getting accustomed to this situation and adapt to it. Still, your posture, bent over the dog, will impress the beagle enough to keep it in its place.

Now the concept of *lie down* will be understood in principle, but you need to refine it by applying it in gradually more difficult situations. The command will come to mean that the beagle is to lie down immediately and to stay down, regardless whether there are other people or other dogs around. Again, the best way to learn this is in a group under the leadership of a good instructor.

"Let Go"

A beagle pup should learn to accept early that at the command *let go* it should allow

Let go. You must convince the beagle pup while it is still young that you are the stronger of the two and that it must give up anything you ask for without protest.

you to take away whatever it is playing with. At first the puppy will growl and try to defend its "booty." This is just the way it behaved with its siblings, against which it had to assert itself to avoid being shoved into the background. In other words, it is a natural reaction, but you should not let it go unchecked. If you do, you will be sorry when it picks up some splintery bone that you must get away from it so it will not be hurt. You must convince the puppy while it is still young that you are the stronger and that it must give up without protest anything you ask for. Practice this first with a toy your puppy is particularly fond of. Get your dog to play with the toy, and then take it away with a curt *"Let go."* Praise its cooperation immediately. Practice with other objects, eventually even with its full dish of food.

Your dog will learn to accept this "game" or will at least not find it unusual to give up whatever it has between its teeth when told to do so. Never use force when practicing this exercise.

"Come"

If you want your beagle to come as soon as you call it, you must take care to avoid a few mistakes at all costs.

✔ Never call your dog to come when you think it likely that it won't do so. If your dog is just learning this concept, it will unlearn it because it gets the idea that your calling can safely be ignored.

✔ Never chase your beagle to catch it if it doesn't respond to your call. Most dogs love to play tag, and your beagle will take your attempts to catch it as an invitation to a game and do its best to keep out of reach. So, do the opposite. Move away from your beagle. Perhaps even squat and hide behind a bush while the dog looks on. This will stimulate the puppy to come to you.

✔ No matter how angry you may get, don't try to correct your dog by yelling at it when it comes up to you. This only scares the dog away. No matter how hard this is for you, control yourself and praise your dog when it comes to you after you called it.

✔ Never call the dog to you when you intend to punish it. Your beagle needs to understand that something pleasant will occur if it comes to you after having been called. The pleasant consequence doesn't always have to be a treat. In fact, I think it better not to reward constantly by feeding treats. You can just as well give a hug, or play with the dog, or simply talk to it in a high, soft voice, giving it praise and strokes.

Make use of those situations when you can safely predict that your dog is going to come toward you. For example, at feeding time, call the dog in a high and friendly tone while you are holding the feeding dish so that the dog can see what you are doing. If it comes, speak to it with praise, stroke it, and then give it the dish with food. Similarly, as you get ready to go out with your dog, you will have little difficulty getting your beagle to come to you. So, make use of all common situations when you know your beagle will want to come toward you in order to teach the concept of *come.* Each time, try everything you can think of to make it worthwhile for your beagle to come to you. This sets up the best conditions for a speedy, pleasant lesson in coming when called.

The beagle belongs to the hound breeds,
which can be split into two groups:
(1) The scent hounds or scent followers
and (2) the sight hounds or sight hunters.

The beagle is by far the best known representative of the scent followers and one of the oldest representatives of the scent-following tracking dogs. The breed probably dates back to pre-Roman times.

In the United States, we recognize two sizes of beagles: 13 inches or under, and over 13 but under 15 inches. The typical weight for a beagle is between 22–40 pounds.

Dog experts often say, correctly, that the beagle is a carbon copy of the harrier and the English foxhound. Both these breeds are considerably larger than the beagle, especially the English foxhound. This makes it all the more important not to breed oversized beagles, meaning individuals that are more than 15 inches. It makes no sense at all to try to turn a beagle into a foxhound!

Although a beagle may have any hound color, most members of the breed are black, white, or tan, with different combinations and

Legend has it that beagles, from the French biegles (meaning small), descended from hounds brought to England by the knights of William the Conqueror.

markings. The coat is close and of medium length and will remain glossy with good daily care. The tail of a healthy beagle is carried gaily, but not curled squirrel style; the ears are set at eye level, drop beside the cheeks, and have "fine leather." The skull is domed and moderately wide, with an indication of peak. The medium-length muzzle should not be snippy. To maintain the true appearance and character traits of the beagle, it is extremely important to breed with the utmost care.

If you want to acquire a beagle and know a dependable pet store or breeder, fine. If not, start by contacting the AKC for assistance (see address on page 90). They will give you the address of the headquarters of the local beagle club. They, in turn, will be more than willing to give you a list of reputable, AKC-approved breeders in your area.

Remember that the beagle has remained popular through the years, despite the competition, because of its many excellent qualities and valued traits. Two of its very outstanding qualities are certainly endurance and courage. It is difficult, perhaps impossible, to find a breed that excels the beagle on these points.

The beagle in the field is almost as well known in America as in Europe, although we know the breed somewhat better as a house pet.

As a house pet, the beagle still distinguishes itself by several excellent qualities. As I said earlier, beagles and children are almost inseparable, and the charming and intelligent beagles are also generally affectionate toward other pets. They are always ready to be on the go, and from excitement and pure joy they often sound their lovely hound voice.

You will have to set limits on this enthusiastic vocalization if you keep a beagle in the city, as you don't want trouble with the neighbors. If you acquire the dog when it is young, you can train it fairly easily even though a beagle, as a natural hunter, derives an unimaginable deal of pleasure from a loud howling session now and then. This is particularly true if it is left alone, but if you start when the dog is young, you shouldn't run into any serious problems.

The beagle is definitely a suitable city hound. It certainly loves to be outside often and will thankfully accept any opportunity to be taken for a walk or to romp out-of-doors. As you walk through the streets, you can depend on the beagle's natural calm as well as its proverbial loyalty. Believe me, the beagle doesn't care at all about bad weather or rough terrain; you can take your dog wherever you want, secure in the knowledge that nothing will wear it down.

If you are a hunter, the beagle is hard to beat. Almost any type of upland game arouses its interest, including cottontail rabbit, squirrel, and pheasant, which are its favorites. If you train the beagle properly, you can derive an enormous amount of pleasure from your helper. Professional trainers often can be of indispensable assistance in developing your beagle as a hunter.

History

Legend has it that beagles, those "merry little hounds with big hearts," descended from hounds used by King Arthur and his knights. Some say their ancestors came to England with William the Conqueror.

It isn't easy, however, to establish exactly when the breed first made its appearance. It is known that the ancient Greeks used so-called scenting hounds for the hunt 400 years or so before Christ. The dogs, which were of several different breeds, hunted in packs with their keepers. In England and Wales this type of hunt was also known about 1400 A.D. The pack consisted not only of scent followers but also included sight hounds, such as greyhounds. In fact, it wasn't until 1550 that people started differentiating among the various types of scent hounds. For example, people trained the large hounds, the so-called buck hounds, to hunt deer and other large game. The small hounds were used to hunt hares, rabbits, and pheasants; and these small dogs were called beighs or beagles, from the French beigle, meaning *small*.

This doesn't mean, however, that the dogs that were called beagles 400 years ago were the same dogs we call beagles today. Representations of beagles from the sixteenth, seventeenth, and eighteenth centuries show that clearly. The dogs varied in height between 5 and 25 inches (13–63.5 cm).

In this connection, it's interesting to note that in the days of King Henry VIII (1491–1547) and even more so during the reign of his daughter, Elizabeth I (1558–1603), the then miniature beagles were transported to the hunting fields in the panniers of saddles or in the pockets of hunting coats.

One supposes that the beagle resulted from experiments in crossing the harrier with the

Southern hound. It is no surprise that in the "early days" beagles were often called "little harriers." Over time, breeders selected the larger individuals from among these dogs, creating a breed that was 19 to 21 inches (48–53.5 cm) in height. Continuous selection, using, in turn, only the smallest individuals for breeding, gradually resulted in a dog of reduced size, a miniature breed called Queen Bess. These dogs proved to be too small for hunting, and they rapidly lost popularity. Breeders continued their experiments, and gradually the first "true" beagle developed in two types: the shallow-flewed and the deep-flewed, depending on the depth of the upper lip. The first type is supposed to have been the faster, and the second, the one with the more musical voice and the more assured manner.

The present-day beagle received a number of characteristics from several other breeds. Its keen nose is supposedly derived from the Kerry beagle, a miniature bloodhound, and all its other traits were acquired by crossing various foxhounds (harriers).

It wasn't until about 1860 that the first well-proportioned beagles were introduced to the United States. One of the known participants was General Richard Rowett of Carlinville, Illinois, who brought several good representatives of the breed from England, including the now famous Rosey and Dolly.

Beagles were known in North America before then, but they were far from ideal individuals, especially in size. The dogs brought over by Rowett and others were used in a professional selective breeding program that resulted in superior beagles within several years. They were able to meet all competitors, including those from England.

It wasn't until 1887, however, that the American/English Beagle Club was formed. The standard of the breed was drafted by General Rowett, Norman Elmore of Granby, Connecticut—famous for his marvelous beagle Ringwood, which also came from England—and Dr. L. H. Twadell of Philadelphia, Pennsylvania. These gentlemen acquitted themselves so well of their task that their standard, with several minor changes, continues to be used today by the National Beagle Club of America. Even the standard used in England differs only slightly from the one devised by the three U.S. pioneers.

Shortly after the turn of the century, the interest in beagles increased to an amazing extent, and many enthusiastic beagle lovers had privately owned packs. Well-known are the Hempstead, Round Hill, Thurnfield, Rockridge, Dungannon, Somerset, Wolver, Piedmont, Old Westbury, and Windholme beagles.

The first beagle field trials were held November 4, 1890, at Hyannis, Massachusetts, and November 7, 1890, at Salem, New Hampshire. Mr. Frank Forest was the winner of the all-age stake for dogs 15 inches and under, and a dog called Tone, owned by the Glenrose Kennels, won the stake for bitches 15 inches and under. Belle Rose, owned by B. S. Turpin, was the winner of the stake for bitches 13 inches and under.

The next year, the number of entries was considerably larger, and from then on one can say that nothing could stop the popularity of the beagle.

Beagles for Work in the Field

Several beagle lovers have made a profession of training beagles for work in the field. Many of these trainers now take their charges over a regular circuit of field trials. They are held

left: The beagle is a natural hunter.

below: Though it is a fairly small dog, the beagle is powerfully built.

almost every weekend throughout the country. Most successful field trial beagles are taken hunting three to five days each week, to remain in top condition for competition.

Your beagle club can tell you where you can find professional trainers. Remember that generally they have more than enough business, so that you will need several names.

At bench shows and field trials, beagles are divided into varieties by size: those not exceeding 13 inches in height at the withers, and those over 13 inches but not exceeding 15 inches.

The size varieties are then further subdivided into specific classes during competition: for field trials these would be 13-inch dogs, 13-inch bitches, 15-inch dogs, and 15-inch bitches. After reading our standards discussion (see pages 86–87), it will be clear that beagles over 15 inches are automatically disqualified from competition.

It certainly would be well worth your time to visit a beagle trial sometime, even if you don't like to hunt. During field trials, beagles are run in braces (meaning pairs). The names of individual hounds are placed on single slips of paper and drawn from a receptacle, the first

beagle drawn running with the second hound drawn, and so on. After all braces have been run, the judges may call back any competing beagle that they wish to see again and brace them in any manner they desire; often they make an animal run a second, third, or even fourth time. I have been at competitions where they made certain dogs run eight times. In the end, all judges will have determined the best performers on that particular occasion.

Most generally, the cottontail rabbit is used as game, although it can happen that hares are used.

You can easily imagine that not all beagles are equally adept at hunting; some may be easily distracted for one reason or another, or become nervous and perform poorly.

A young beagle with true determination is just about the ideal hound. Its natural desire to hunt constitutes the germ for success, with the proper training. The trainer tries to get the beagle to follow a comparatively cold trail until the quarry has gone to earth or has been

above: Even pups are curious and adventuresome, and can easily get into trouble.

below: This beagle is very attentive and can be taught many skills.

Scale of Points

	Points	Total
Head		
Skull	5	
Ears	10	
Eyes	5	
Muzzle	5	25
Body		
Neck	5	
Chest and shoulders	15	
Back, loin, and ribs	15	35
Running Gear		
Forelegs	10	
Hips, thighs, and		
hind legs	10	
Feet	10	30
Coat	5	
Stern	5	10
		100

Varieties

There shall be two varieties: the 13 inch, which shall be for hounds not exceeding 13 inches in height, and the 15 inch, which shall be for hounds over 13 but not exceeding 15 inches in height.

Disqualification

Any hound measuring more than 15 inches shall be disqualified.

caught. The young beagle must be the type to enjoy working in rough, unknown territory, regardless of the weather.

It is safe to say that a good beagle thrives on work, and the more it goes hunting with its master and its pack, the more it enjoys the chase. Even if you don't hunt, I think it will still be an unforgettable experience to see a pack of bea-gles hunt. They truly deserve the name I heard somewhere: music makers of the meadows.

Beagle Shows

Every year there are local and regional shows for beagle hounds. Using the breed standard as a basis, the judges evaluate and grade beagles on their general appearance, physique, bearing, and behavior. Beagles are shown in two separate varieties. At the AKC point show, they are divided by sex into classes, from which the first-place winners advance to the Winners class. It is from the Winners class that the judge selects his one best class dog (and later his one best class bitch) of each breed or variety to receive the point awards championship for the day.

The AKC judges place the hounds first through fourth in the classes, then select their Winners, Best of Breed, Best of Winners, and BOS (Best of Opposite Sex). Beagle shows (or dog shows, in general) offer a wealth of information. Manufacturers of dog foods offer samples of the latest brands, usually at no or little cost. Useful accessories for beagle owners are also on display. Contacts with other beagle owners are quickly formed, and a lively exchange of experience and information is soon underway. The judges give tips and suggestions for the care and management of your beagle.

If you would like to enter your beagle in an AKC show, check the AKC events calendar for information, and then contact the show superintendent for a copy of the premium list which includes the appropriate entry forms. Blank official AKC entry forms can also be obtained from the AKC and kept on file for use in a pinch. But to enter any show you must mail the complete filled out and signed forms, with

the appropriate fees, to the show superintendent for that specific show.

Description and Standard (AKC)

Head: The skull should be fairly long, slightly domed at occiput, with cranium broad and full.

Ears: Ears set on moderately low, long, reaching when drawn out nearly, if not quite, to the end of the nose; fine in texture, fairly broad—with almost complete absence of erectile power—setting close to the head, with the forward edge slightly inturning to the cheek—rounded at tip.

Eyes: Eyes large, set well apart; soft and houndlike; expression gentle and pleading; of a brown or hazel color.

Muzzle: Muzzle of medium length, straight and square-cut; the stop moderately defined.

Jaws: Level. Lips free from flews; nostrils large and open.

Defects: A very flat skull, narrow across the top; excess of dome; eyes small, sharp, and terrier-like or prominent and protruding; muzzle long, snippy or cut away decidedly below the eyes, or very short. Roman-nosed, or upturned, giving a dish-faced expression. Ears short, set on high or with a tendency to rise above the point of origin.

Body, neck, and throat: Neck rising free and light from the shoulders, strong in substance yet not loaded, of medium length. The throat clean and free from folds of skin; a slight wrinkle below the angle of the jaw, however, may be allowable.

Defects: A thick, short neck carried on a line with the top of the shoulders. Throat showing dewlap and folds of skin to a degree termed "throatiness."

Shoulders and chest: Shoulders sloping, clean, muscular, not heavy or loaded—conveying the idea of freedom of action with activity and strength. Chest deep and broad, but not broad enough to interfere with the free play of the shoulders.

Defects: Straight, upright shoulders. Chest disproportionately wide or with lack of depth.

Back, loin, and ribs: Back short, muscular, and strong. Loin broad and slightly arched, and the ribs well sprung, giving abundance of lung room.

Defects: Very long, swayed, or roached back. Flat, narrow loin. Flat ribs.

Forelegs: Straight, with plenty of bone in proportion to size of the hound. Pasterns short and straight.

Feet: Close, round, and firm. Pad full and hard.

Defects: Out at elbows. Knees knuckled over forward or bent backward. Forelegs crooked or dachshund-like. Feet long, open, or spreading.

Hips, thighs, hind legs, and feet: Hips and thighs strong and well muscled, giving abundance of propelling power. Stifles strong and well let down. Hocks firm, symmetrical, and moderately bent. Feet close and firm.

Defects: Cowhocks or straight hocks. Lack of muscle and propelling power. Open feet.

Tail: Set moderately high; carried gaily, but not turned forward over the back; with slight curve; short compared with size of the hound; with brush.

Defects: A long tail. Teapot curve or inclined forward from the root. Rat tail with absence of brush.

Coat: A close, hard, hound coat of medium length.

Defects: A short, thin coat, or of a soft quality.

Color: Any true hound color.

General appearance: A miniature foxhound, solid and big for its inches, with the wear-and-tear look of the hound that can last in the chase and follow its quarry to the death.

Love implies care and whatever care you lavish on your dogs will be returned by them many times over.

Beagle puppies thrive with love and affection. They are very responsive and make wonderful companions.

One way to show off your beagle is to enter it in dog shows.

Organizations and Clubs

American Boarding Kennel Association
4575 Galley Road, Suite 400-A
Colorado Springs, CO 80915

American Humane Association
9725 East Hampton Avenue
Denver, CO 80231

American Kennel Club
260 Madison Avenue
New York, NY 10016
Web site: *http://www.AKC.org*
For Registration, Records, Litter Information:
5580 Centerview Drive
Raleigh, NC 27606

American Veterinary Medical Association
930 North Meacham Road
Schaumburg, IL 60173

Canadian Kennel Club
111 Eglington Avenue
Toronto 12
Ontario, Canada

Canine Eye Registry Foundation (CERF)
South Campus Court, Building C
West Lafayette, IN 47907

Institute for Genetic Disease Control (GDC)
P.O. Box 222
Davis, CA 95617

National Beagle Club*
8 Baldwin Place
Westport, CT 06880

National Dog Registry (tattoo, microchip)
P.O. Box 116
Woodstock, NY 12498

Orthopedic Foundation for Animals (OFA)
2300 Nifong Boulevard
Columbia, MO 65201

Owner-Handler Association of America
583 Knoll Court
Seaford, NY 11783

Periodicals

AKC Gazette
260 Madison Avenue
New York, NY 10016

Dog Fancy Magazine
P.O. Box 53264
Boulder, CO 80322-3264

Dog World
29 North Wacker Drive
Chicago, IL 60606

Gaines Touring with Towser
(a directory of hotels and motels that accom-
  modate guests with dogs.)
P.O. Box 5700
Kankakee, IL 60902

*Addresses may change as new officers are elected. The latest listing can always be obtained from the American Kennel Club.

Books

In addition to the most recent edition of the official publication of the AKC, *The Complete Dog Book,* published by Howell Book House, Inc., in New York, the following publications contain useful information.

Alderton, David. *The Dog Care Manual.* Hauppauge, New York: Barron's Educational Series, Inc., 1986.

American Animal Hospital Association. *Encyclopedia of Dog Health and Care.* New York: The Philip Lief Group, Inc., 1994.

Animal Medical Center. *The Complete Book of Dog Health.* New York: Howell Book House, 1985.

Baer, Ted. *Communicating with Your Dog.* Hauppauge, New York: Barron's Educational Series, Inc., 1994.

Clark, Ross D., and Joan R. Strainer. *Medical and Genetic Aspects of Purebred Dogs.* Fairway, Kansas, and St. Simons Island, Georgia: Forum Publications, Inc., 1994.

Coile, Caroline D. *Encyclopedia of Dog Breeds.* Hauppauge, New York: Barron's Educational Series, Inc., 1998.

Klever, Ulrich. *The Complete Book of Dog Care.* Hauppauge, New York: Barron's Educational Series, Inc., 1989.

Lorenz, Konrad. *Man Meets Dog.* London and New York: Penguin Books, 1967.

Pinney, Cristopher. *Guide to Home Pet Grooming.* Hauppauge, New York: Barron's Educational Series, Inc., 1990.

Ullman, Hans-J., and Evamaria Ullman. *The New Dog Handbook.* Hauppauge, New York: Barron's Educational Series, Inc., 1985.

Wrede, Barbara. *Civilizing Your Puppy.* Hauppauge, New York: Barron's Educational Series, Inc., 1992.

Important Note

This pet owner's guide tells the reader how to buy and care for beagles. The author and the publisher consider it important to point out that the advice given in the book is meant primarily for normally developed puppies from a good breeder—that is, dogs of excellent physical health and good character.

Anyone who adopts a fully grown dog should be aware that the animal has already formed its basic impressions of human beings. The new owner should watch the animal carefully, including its behavior toward humans, and should meet the previous owner. If the dog comes from a shelter, it may be possible to get some information on the dog's background and peculiarities there. There are dogs that as a result of bad experiences with humans behave in an unnatural manner or may even bite. Only people who have experience with dogs should take in such an animal. Even well-behaved and carefully supervised dogs sometimes do damage to someone else's property or cause accidents. It is therefore in the owner's interest to be adequately insured against such eventualities, and we strongly urge all dog owners to purchase a liability policy that covers their dog.

Caution is further advised in the association of children with dogs, in meetings with other dogs, and in exercising the dog without a leash.

Make certain that the dog bed you choose is large enough for a full-grown beagle to lie down in comfortably.

Choosing the correct food for puppies and adult dogs will result in glowing health.

All beagles should be exercised every day. An obese dog loses its natural resistance, and its life span is likely to be short.

below: Always praise your pup for its successful efforts.

Beagles love to observe what's going on.

I N D E X

American Kennel Club
(AKC), 7–8, 81, 86, 90
Anal sacs, 62–63

Baldness, 62
Bathing, 38–39
Bed, 18
Birth, 53–56
Bites, 69
Boarding kennel, 19–21
Breeder, 7–10
Breeding, 5–6, 50
Breed standard, 81, 87
Brushing, 39
Buying:
considerations before,
5–11
male vs. female, 5–6

Carbohydrates, 42–43
Cesarean operations, 56
Chest, 87
Chewing, 18
Children, 23
Clipping of nails, 30–31
Coat:
breed standard, 87
care of, 38–39
disorders of, 61–62
puppy, 10
Colostrum, 46, 56–57
"Come," 78–79
Constipation, 62
Coronavirus, 69
Crate, 15

Diarrhea, 62
Diet. See also Feeding;
Food
carbohydrates, 42–43
fats, 43
meat, 41–42
minerals, 43
oils, 43
vitamins, 43, 46
Digestive disorders, 62–63
Distemper, 66

Dog biscuits, 42, 44
Doghouse, 18–19
Dog shows, 86–87

Ear(s):
breed standard, 87
care of, 31–34
Ear mites, 34
Eczema, 61–62
Equipment, 26–27
Estrus, 49–50
Euthanasia, 71
Eye disorders, 70

False pregnancy, 51
Fats, 43
Feeding. See also Diet;
Food
growing dogs, 47
grown dog, 47
pregnant dams, 47
puppy, 45–47, 56–59
supplementary, 46–47, 59
Feet:
breed standard, 87
care of, 29–30
Female, 5–6
Field trials, 83–86
First aid, 69–70
Fleas, 34, 62
Food, 43–45
Frostbite, 70

Grains, 42
Grooming:
equipment for, 26–27
foot care, 29–30
nails, 30–31
teeth, 29

Head, 87
Heartworms, 65
Heat. see Estrus
Heating, 53, 58
"Heel," 74–75
Hepatitis, 66–67
History, 82–83

Hookworms, 65
Housebreaking, 14–15

Identification tag, 26
Information resources,
90–91
Insect stings, 70

Kennel:
boarding, 19–21
puppy, 10–11
Kennel cough, 65

Lactation, 46–47, 56–57
Leash, 26
Leptospirosis, 67
"Let go," 78
Lice, 35
"Lie down," 75, 78
Lyme disease, 34–35

Male, 5–6, 50
Mating, 50
Meat, 41–42
Meconium, 55–56
Milk, 41–42
Minerals, 43
Mites, 34, 62

Nails, 30–31
Neck, 87
Nursing, 56–57
Nutrition. See Diet; Food

Obedience training, 73–79
Oils, 43
Organizations, 90

Paper training, 15
Parvovirus, 69
Pregnancy:
description of, 50–51
feeding during, 47
preparations for, 51–53
Protein, 41–42
Pseudorabies, 69
Pulse, 71

Puppy:
birth of, 53–56
bringing home, 11
caring for, 57–59
feeding of, 45–47, 56–59
first days with, 17
first visit with, 9
opening of eyes, 58–59
private spot for, 17–18
selection of, 10–11
training of, 14–15
weaning of, 59
weight of, 51

Rabies, 68
Rocky Mountain spotted
fever, 35
Roundworms, 64
Run, 19

Shampoo, 26, 38–39
Shoulders, 87
Shows, 86–87
"Sit," 73–74
Skin disorders, 61–62
Space, 6–7
"Stay," 74
Stud, 50

Tail, 87
Tapeworms, 63–64
Teeth, 29
Ticks, 35
Toys, 22–23
Training:
obedience, 73–79
puppy, 14–15
Traveling, 22

Vaccinations, 67
Vitamins, 43, 46

Weaning, 59
Whelping box, 52–53, 58
Whipworms, 65
Worming, 59, 63
Worms, 63–65

About the Author

Lucia E. Parent has written extensively on canine topics. She is also the author of books on hamsters and other small mammals. *Beagles* is her first dog book for Barron's. She is also the author of Barron's *The New Rabbit Handbook.*

For my daughter Tanya, with love.

Photo Credits

Barbara Augello: pages 2–3, 4, 9, 13, 16, 25 (top right), 29, 41, 48, 60, 64, 68, 73, 80, 85 (bottom), 93 (bottom left and right); Norvia Behling: pages 8 (top and bottom), 24 (top right), 33 (top left), 45, 49, 69; Kent and Donna Dannen: pages 20, 21 (left), 25 (top left), 32 (bottom), 52, 56 (bottom), 57, 85 (top); Tara Darling: pages 24 (top left), 37, 76 (top), 81, 84 (both), 88 (bottom right); Karen Hudson: pages 17, 32 (top left), 33 (bottom right), 61, 89 (bottom); Pets by Paulette: pages 5, 12 (all 3), 21 (right), 24 (bottom), 25 (bottom), 28, 32 (top right), 33 (top right and bottom left), 36, 40, 44, 53, 56 (top), 65, 72, 76 (bottom), 77, 88 (top and bottom left), 89 (top), 92 (both), 93 (top).

Cover Photos

Front and back covers: Norvia Behling; inside front and back covers: Pets by Paulette.

Acknowledgment

Special thanks to my daughter, Tanya M. Heming-Vriends, for sharing her exceptional knowledge. I'm also grateful to the biologist Dr. Matthew M. Vriends, who brings more than 40 years of experience to the field; he was most helpful in the preparation of this revised third edition. I'm thankful as well to my editor, Pat Hunter, of Barron's. All the opinions and conclusions expressed in this book are my own, however, and any errors must be my own responsibility.

L.E.P.

All inquiries should be addressed to:
Barron's Educational Series, Inc.
250 Wireless Boulevard
Hauppauge, NY 11788
http://www.barronseduc.com

International Standard Book No. 0-7641-2002-6

Library of Congress Catalog Card No. 2002035610

Library of Congress Cataloging-in-Publication Data
Parent, Lucia E.
    Beagles / Lucia E. Parent.—3rd ed.
        p. cm. — (A Complete pet owner's manual)
        Includes bibliographical references (p.).
        ISBN 0-7641-2002-6
        1. Beagles (Dog breed) I. Title. II. Series.

SF429.B3 P35 2003
636.753'7—dc21   2002035610

Printed in China
9 8 7 6 5 4 3 2 1